D1568129

FRIDA PONTÉN

Crochet for the Fun of It

TRAFALGAR SQUARE
North Pomfret, Vermont

Table of Contents

First published in the United States of America in 2011 by
Trafalgar Square Books
North Pomfret, Vermont 05053

Originally published in Norwegian as Hekleglede by Cappelen Damm A/S

© 2008 Cappelen Damm A/S
English translation © 2011 Trafalgar Square Books

ISBN: 978-1-57076-456-1

Library of Congress Control Number: 2010935680

Translation by Carol Huebscher Rhoades
Book design by Ellen Renberg
Cover design by R.M. Didier
Photographs by Erika Likén

Printed in China

HAPPY

PASTELS

3

I want
this
crochet
book
to be
easy to
under-
stand!

Preface

I always become so entranced whenever I go into a yarn store – The yarn is so enticing and there are so many different types to choose from – and I would like to have almost all of them. So, I end up buying new yarn, new knitting and crochet patterns, needles and hooks (because I can never find mine), and then hurry home, sit down on the sofa and begin a new project! Everything is fine and dandy and I can imagine how nice I will look in the new sweater. Just like when I told myself how great I would look in the socks, mittens, cardigans, and all the other garments that will never be completed…and that is the root of my problem. I just can't understand what is written in the patterns. It's like another language to me, I try to understand but I can see what I'm making is totally wrong and I give up.

It's the reason why yarn falls on my head every time I open a closet door at my house. Every fall, I sort the yarns by color into smooth baskets so I can at least display them decoratively. Not such a bad idea either as they look really nice!

One day I sat down and put my mind to crochet and decided it would be quite easy to copy the style of a finished garment, so I thought I'd try a sweater. I took out a sweater that fit well, laid it flat on a table and crocheted a front that was exactly the same size! I had to make sure that the shaping on the two garments matched throughout to ensure that it would be right! Before I knew it, I had actually finished my first crocheted garment! And then I began to crochet many things that also got finished. When I had my last baby, I thought I could try to crochet some little things (and little things go so quickly!). Of course I forged ahead but I also learned to ask questions about things I didn't understand— the local yarn shop owners are skillful knitters and crocheters and are willing to help. Don't be afraid to ask for help.

I want this crochet book to be easy to understand. If you have never crocheted before, you should start with something easy – for example, the bracelet or scarf. Make sure that you begin with small quick things so you'll finish your projects. And, even if you only crochet scarves and leg warmers for everyone you know, they make wonderful gifts! Your friends will certainly be happy when they receive something lovely that you crocheted for them.

What's so exciting about fashion today is that you can once again wear lots of colors. Crochet a bright yellow scarf and a matching yellow hat? Or try something with purple, green and orange. Make yourself noticed in a variety of bright colors. Use yarns you already have as a lot of these projects take a small amount of yarn, don't be afraid to mix and match colors and textures.

I hope that you find lots of inspiration in this book and that you can set aside some time to crochet. If you become a real crochet enthusiast, you'll discover that it is the world's best therapy. Good luck.

Frida Pontén

HAPPY!

Colorful Button Brooches

Materials:
Various size buttons; smooth cotton yarn, crochet hook suitable for yarn; sewing thread and needle; fiber fill.

Instructions:
Make sure that you crochet tightly enough that the buttons aren't visible through the crochet.

1. Crochet a flat circle and place it securely over a button, working as follows: Begin with ch 4; join into a ring with slip st.

2. Increase by crocheting 2 sc in each st of previous rnd for the first 2-3 rnds. Now decide how much you need to increase. Usually increasing in every other st works well. When the circle is big enough, end with 3-4 slip sts so that the circle is finished evenly. Make the circle about ¼ in / .5 cm bigger than the button so that you can fold down an edge all around the circle. Stuff the circle with fiber fill (or yarn in the same color) so that the brooch is soft and convex. Secure with sewing thread behind the button – see drawing.

3. Sew the brooch securely to jacket or fasten with a safety pin on the back.

Fold the crochet edge over to back of the button.

Stitch here to bring in the crocheted circle so that it surrounds and firmly holds the button.

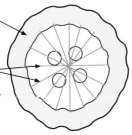

Make an old jacket like new again with some colorful button brooches.

Hair Accessory

Materials:
Leftover yarn, crochet hook suitable for yarn, hair pins or elastic, buttons, sewing thread and needle.

Instructions:
Small Flower
1. Ch 3; turn. Insert hook into the 2nd ch and sc 1. Ch 2; turn.

2. 3 sc and ch 2; turn.

3. 4 sc, ch 1; turn. Repeat this row once more.

4. 4 sc; turn.

5. 3 sc; turn.

6. 2 sc; turn.

7. 1 sc and finish off: cut yarn and bring tail through last loop.

I crocheted a total of 6 petals for this flower. I arranged the petals and sewed them together with matching sewing thread. Sew a pretty button to the center of the flower with matching sewing thread.

Attach a small flat hair pin or elastic to the flower with a few stitches. You can also glue a small round piece of matching color felt or fabric to the back so it will also look nice!

If you want to make bigger flowers, you only have to increase more before you begin the decreases. You can decorate the flowers with smooth beads or smooth embroidery yarn as I did on the two large flowers!

Yellow Mohair Scarf

Materials:
Yellow fuzzy mohair yarn, needles US size 19 / 15 mm, matching yellow cotton yarn and crochet hook suitable for yarn.

Instructions:
1. With mohair and knitting needles, CO 12 sts loosely.

2. Work in stockinette.

3. Knit the scarf as long as you want. Mine is 55 in / 140 cm long.

4. BO rather loosely as follows: K2, *pass the right st over the left st on the right needle. K1*. Rep * to *. Weave in all tails neatly on WS.

5. With cotton yarn and hook, crochet a row of sc across end of scarf. The stitch count should be a multiple of 4 – I had 24 sc for mine. Ch 1 and turn.

6. *Ch 10 and sl st into the 4th sc. Rep from * across. Turn.

7. Around each chain loop, work: 6 sc around chain loop, ch 5 and sl st into 1 st ch, 6 sc. Ch 1 between each loop and crochet around each loop the same way. Cut yarn and weave in tails on WS.

With holes all over, you'll easily find a place to pin a colorful brooch

Pink and Red Striped Leg Warmers

Materials:
Warm wool yarn in two soft colors; crochet hook suitable for yarn (I used hook US size G-6 / 4 mm, needle and thread to match yarn.

Instructions:
1. Ch as many sts as needed for the leg warmer to go around your foot and leg. I worked with 40 sts. Work 2 rows in sc; turn each row with ch 2.

2. Now dc into every sc across; turn each row with ch 2. I worked 2 rows dc in one color and then changed color. Continue in dc to desired length (My leg warmer is 13 ½ in / 34 cm long). Finish the leg warmer with 2 rows sc.

3. With RS facing RS, seam leg warmers with a doubled strand of matching sewing thread; turn so RS faces out.

Leg warmers are a wonderful little extra.

I have lots of yarn in my baskets — a great inspiration for starting new and exciting projects!

Tweed Wrist Warmers with Flower

Materials:
Thick tweed yarn; crochet hook US size M/N-13 / 9 mm or size suitable for yarn; lurex yarn with glitter for flower in a matching color; needle and thread.

Instructions:
1. Ch as many sts as needed to go around your wrist/hand. Work back and forth in single crochet and turn each row with ch 1. Note: I worked each sc into the back loop to make a striped pattern.

2. Crochet wrist warmer to desired length (mine are 3 ¼ in / 8 cm long).

3. Crochet the flower with lurex yarn: Ch 8 and join into a ring with a slip st. Work as many sc into ring as will fit.

4. *Ch 6 (approx) and join the chain with a sl st to one of the sc. Rep from * around, making a total of 5 petals. Space petals as evenly as possible. Sc around each chain loop so that the petals hold their shape. Sew the flowers securely to wrist warmers with small stitches.

Squiggly Scarf

Materials:
4 different types of yarn: smooth lurex, tweed wool, single color wool and a smooth cotton; crochet hook suitable for yarn.

Instructions:

1. Ch a long cord about 39 in / 1 meter long.

2. Turn and work 3 sc or 3 dc into each chain. If you are using dc, the squiggly scarf will be longer. Work all sts rather loosely. Cut yarn and weave in ends. Crochet more cords in various colors. Make all the cords the same length and wrap them together for a scarf. If you want a winter scarf, increase the length of each cord and make several of the cords with heavier yarn so the scarf will be thick and warm!

On one of the squiggly cords, I first crocheted (with sc) following steps 1 and 2 above and then I changed yarn, turned, and worked in sc across with smooth pink lurex yarn. Experiment with different types of yarn and colors!

Lemons arranged
in a lovely
crocheted bowl
makes an attractive
centerpiece.

Flower Bowl

Materials:
Medium weight cotton yarn in 7 different colors and crochet hook US size D-3 / 3 mm; starch = wallpaper paste; a large bowl to form the crocheted bowl around.

Instructions:
Flower
1. Ch 7 and join into a ring with sl st.

2. *1 sc around ring (do not insert hook into ch sts but around ring), ch 4; rep from * 6 more times and then work 1 sc around ring, ch 2 and 1 hdc into first sc.

3. *Ch 5, then 1 sc around chain loop. Rep from * 6 more times and then work ch 2 and 1 dc into hdc of row below.

4. *Ch 7 and then 1 sc around chain loop. Rep from * 6 more times and then ch 3, 1 tr into dc.

5. *Ch 8 and then 1 sc around chain loop. Rep from * 6 more times and then ch 8, 1 sl st into tr.

6. Work around each chain loop as follows: 1 sc, 1 hdc, 4 dc, ch 5 (join this "picot" into first ch with sl st), 4 dc, 1 hdc, 1 sc.

Make as many flowers as you want. My bowl has 7 flowers and

is 11 ¾ in / 30 cm in diameter and about 6 in / 15 cm high. Use matching sewing thread to join all the flowers, securing ends well.

Dip the bowl into the paste (mix as directed on package), place over an upside down bowl and let dry.

Carefully loosen the crocheted bowl when it is completely dry.

Colorful
Bed Throw

Materials:

An assortment of doilies and potholders in many colors from a flea market or if you are lucky your grandmother's stash; matching sewing thread.

Instructions:

1. Lay out all the doilies and potholders on the floor and move them around until you are happy with the arrangement.

2. Join the pieces with sewing thread. If there is too much space between pieces, you can crochet chain cords between pieces to hold them together.

Flea market finds and great-grandmother's old doilies and potholders make a fun bedspread.

Two-color
pattern
knitting
isn't the
easiest
project to
begin with.
However,
if you steam
press your
work under
a damp
cotton
cloth, the
knitting
will smooth
out evenly.

Knit-Patterned Scarf
(And a little crochet)

Materials:
Alpaca yarn "Mirasol" (100% alpaca, 137 yds / 125 m per 50 g). I used three colors: gray tweed, bright turquoise, and heathery petroleum blue. Knitting needles and crochet hook suitable for yarn.

Instructions:
1. With gray yarn, CO 53 sts and purl 1 row. Turn.

2. Continue in stockinette, working in charted pattern.

3. Work the charted rows 2 times so that the knitting matches that in the photo.

4. BO to match knitting tension. If the scarf pulls in, you've bound off too tightly; if the edge is wavy, then you've bound off too loosely. Weave in all tails on WS. Make another pattern section the same way for the other end of the scarf.

5. With gray, work 1 row of sc across lower edge of pattern-knitted piece; turn with ch 1 in turquoise yarn and then work 2 rows sc. Finish off and weave in tails.

6. With gray, work 1 row sc. Cut yarn. Repeat steps 5 and 6 on the other patterned section.

7. Now work in dc (turning all rows with ch 2) with the bright turquoise yarn to desired length. The turquoise section on my scarf is 31 ½ in / 80 cm long. Cut yarn and weave in ends. Join to the other pattern-knitted piece by crocheting sections together.

8. Steam press the entire scarf on WS. Check the yarn ball band for correct iron temperature.

If the WS of the pattern-knitted sections looks a little messy, you can make a lining. Use a thin fabric in a color that matches the scarf. Fold under all the edges of the fabric (miter corners) and sew carefully to the back of the scarf with very small stitches on WS.

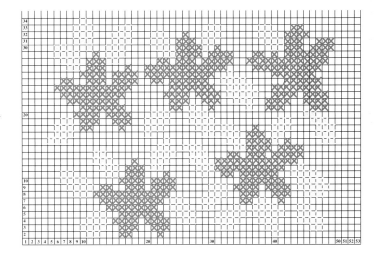

Chart is 1 repeat in length of pattern. Work the charted rows twice so that your scarf matches that in the photo.

□ = gray

= bright turquoise

✕ = heathery petroleum blue

PASTELS

Crocheted Edging for a Sweater

Update an old knitted sweater by adding a crocheted cuff. I cut both sleeves off at the same length and then made a double crochet edging!

Materials:
Tweed ribbon yarn, crochet hook suitable for yarn, a knitted sweater.

Instructions:
1. Cut off sleeve to desired length and unravel so that there is a complete round of live stitches all around the row where you will crochet.

2. Work 1 sc into each knit st around. It is important that you crochet rather tightly. If you crochet too loosely, the sleeve edge will be wavy; too tightly, however, and you might not be able to get your hand through the sleeve. Join end of rnd to beg with sl st.

3. Ch 3, yarn over hook and dc into the 2nd st. Ch 1, skip 1 sc and continue with dc around. Now work as many rnds as you like. Work ch 3 instead of dc as first st of each new rnd.

Use a contrast color, so that your lovely edging will stand out.

Net-Crocheted Square Shawl

Materials:
Pale pink "Misti" (100% alpaca, 55 yds / 50 m per 50 g); crochet hook US size K-10 ½ / 7 mm; large smooth, mother-of-pearl buttons for edging and matching sewing thread.

Instructions:
1. Ch as many sts as needed for a shawl to go around your shoulders well. My shawl is 51 ¼ × 23 ¾ in / 130 × 60 cm.

2. Now work in net pattern with dc: turn, yarn around hook and insert hook into the 5th st from end = 1st dc. Ch 1, yarn around hook to begin dc, skip 1 ch, 1 dc, *ch 1, skip 1 ch, 1 dc; rep from * across.
   Turn all rows with ch 4. Always dc into dc of row below.

3. When shawl is desired length, work 2 rows of sc all around the shawl to make the edging more "solid."

4. Securely sew buttons onto short sides of shawl.

A lovely and cozy shawl for those cool spring evenings.

Flower Brooch

Materials:
White cotton yarn, crochet hook suitable for yarn, needle and thread, safety pin.

Instructions:

1. Ch 8 and join into a ring with sl st.

2. Crochet the flower petals as follows: Into ring, work: I sc, I hdc, I dc, I hdc, I sc = I petal. Note: these sts are all worked around the ring, not into chain sts. Work a total of 5 petals the same way. End with sl st into first sc. If you have trouble fitting all the petals into the ring, push the sts to make room for the rest.

3. *Ch 4 and join with sl st to the sc between two petals of the previous rnd. Rep from *around to make the bases for the next round of petals.

4. Now work I sc, I hdc, 4 dc, I hdc, I sc into each chain loop around. The sections between the stars are also a flower petal group.

5. Ch 5 and join with sl st to sc between petals of previous rnd as in step 3.

6. Into each chain loop work: *I sc, I hdc, 3 dc, ch 3 (join the last ch to top of dc under the chain so that you have a "picot" at the tip of the petal), 3 dc, I hdc, I sc; rep from * around.

7. Weave in yarn tails on WS. Sew flower wherever you like on the scarf.

(For the scarf you could use the pattern on page II, add beads instead of an edging)

This flower brooch looks lovely on a mohair scarf with beads sewn on the edges.

Egg Cozies

Materials:
Sport weight wool yarn and crochet hook suitable for yarn (I used US size G-6 / 4 mm), scraps of printed fabric; fiber fill.

Instructions:
1. Chain as many sts as needed to go around an egg; join into a ring with sl st.

2. Rnd 2: Sc into each ch around.

3. Rnd 3: Sc into back loop of each sc around for a pattern line. Work following the rnds the same way.

4. Shape top when cozy is long enough: dec 4 sts evenly spaced around.

5. Rnd 5: Work as for rnd 3.

6. Dec 4 sts evenly spaced around.

7. Dec around on every 3rd st until no sts remain. You can join the little hole at the top with the yarn tail. You can then sew a bead to the top or make a little soft "button" as I did.

8. Fabric ball: Cut out a circle about 1 ½-1 ¾ in / 4-4.5 cm in diameter from the patterned fabric. With very small stitches and a doubled strand of sewing thread, sew running stitch about ¼ in / a few mm in from the edge all around the circle. Pull the thread at both ends to draw the fabric into a little bowl. Stuff with fiber fill. Pull the threads tight so that the circle now forms a ball and secure the thread with a safety pin. Sew the ball to the tip of the egg cozy. Sew up into the ball so that the stitches on the underside are invisible. Sew with very small stitches and fasten off ends securely.

No more cold eggs for those who sleep in on a weekend morning.

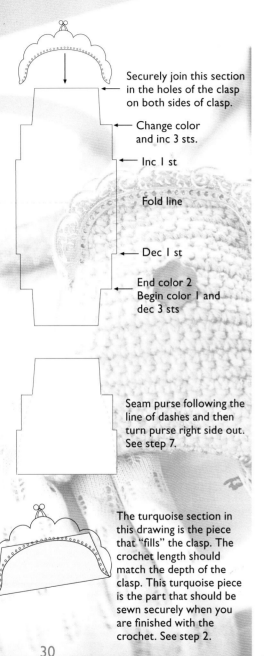

Securely join this section in the holes of the clasp on both sides of clasp.

Change color and inc 3 sts.

Inc 1 st

Fold line

Dec 1 st

End color 2
Begin color 1 and dec 3 sts

Seam purse following the line of dashes and then turn purse right side out. See step 7.

The turquoise section in this drawing is the piece that "fills" the clasp. The crochet length should match the depth of the clasp. This turquoise piece is the part that should be sewn securely when you are finished with the crochet. See step 2.

30

Change Purse

Materials:

Cotton yarn, matching color thin lurex thread (cotton and lurex held together through-out), crochet hook suitable for yarn, purse clasp, sewing thread in matching color, needle and smooth mother-of-pearl button.

Instructions:

1. Ch as many sts as needed to go around the clasp. For my purse, I used slightly heavy cotton yarn held together with yellow and pink lurex thread. I crocheted with hook US size G-6 / 4 mm and began with ch 15; my purse is 3 ¾ in / 8 cm wide.

2. Work in sc and turn each row with ch 1. Work until sc section is same length as clasp depth. When the clasp is "full" of sc rows, begin shaping on both sides – see drawing.

3. Increase row: With new color, ch 3 and crochet into the 4th st of the first crocheted section. Work in sc across and end the row with ch 4. Turn and sc back.

4. Work 3 rows of sc (= approx ¾ in / 2 cm) and then work an increase row: inc 1 st at each side = ch 2 and turn so that you have 1 new st. Work in sc for 3 ¼-4 in / 8-10 cm. Now you are

at the bottom of the purse and fold line.

5. Now work in reverse to match front of purse. Work in sc for 3 ¼-4 in / 8-10 cm and then, on next row, dec 1 st at each side. Crochet about ¾ in / 2 cm with this stitch count. End this color; cut yarn, and weave in tails.

6. Begin with the first color again but begin in the 4th st. End when piece matches beginning section. Cut yarn and weave in tails.

7. Fold the crochet at the center. Seam along the edges with small stitches in matching doubled strand of sewing thread. Do not seam the section that will be sewn onto the clasp. Make sure there will be a "straight" edge when you turn the piece right side out and not a stair step edge that crochet can some-times have! See drawing.

8. Turn the purse right side out and sew the front and back to the clasp. I used a doubled strand of thread to sew twice around so that the join was very firm.

9. Securely attach a smooth mother-of-pearl button at the center.

I found a
clasp that
I fell in
love with,
all I had
to do was
get going
on my own
special
change
purse.

Narrow Crocheted Band for a Beige Cardigan

Materials:
Knitted cardigan and thin lilac yarn, crochet hook suitable for yarn.

Instructions:
1. Work 1 row of sc around the front and neck opening of the wrap cardigan. You might also want to make the same edging around the ends of the sleeves and lower edge of cardigan.

2. Next row: *1 sc, 1 hdc, 1 dc, 1 tr, 1 dc, 1 hdc, 1 sc; rep from * around. Cut yarn and weave in tails.

Crocheted Squiggly Scarf

This scarf is more like a necklace than a scarf.

Materials
Lustrous smooth heather yarn and crochet hook suitable for yarn.

Instructions
1. Ch a long cord about 59 in / 150 cm long.

2. Turn and work 3 sc into each chain.

3. Cut yarn and weave in tails.

Make a boring beige sweater stand out by adding a pretty crocheted edging and a lovely scarf.

Pink Pillows with White Doilies

Materials:
Pillows and pillow cases, crocheted doilies, needle and thread.

If you're lucky, you'll find some pretty crocheted doilies in grandmother's linen cupboard or at a flea market!

Instructions:
With matching thread, sew the doilies onto the pillow case with small invisible stitches. Cut thread and voila – it's done!

So elegant and easy!

Round Rag Rug

Materials:
Strips of cotton fabric; large crochet hook. I used US size NP-15/ 10 mm.

Crocheting with fabric strips isn't difficult but it can be heavy work, so you'll need some muscle power! I usually hold the crochet hook with both hands to manage it. It is easier to crochet with thinner strips but then the rug won't be as strong. I used strips about 1 ¼ in / 3.5 cm wide for a thick and strong mat.

Instructions:
1. Ch 5 and join into a ring with sl st.

2. Work 2 or 3 sc in each chain around. On the following rnds, experiment to see how much to increase. If the mat is bowl-shaped, you haven't increased enough; if it is loose and wavy, you added too many stitches. I laid the rug out on the floor after each round to make sure it lay flat. You should also place the mat a little away from you so that you can check to make sure the color combinations are as nice as you imagined.

3. Change colors as often as you like. Mix single color strips with patterned ones to make the rug livelier.

4. End mat with 4-5 sl sts to round off the final row. Cut strips and weave in tails.

A colorful mat for the bathroom floor, it will keep your feet warm on cold mornings.

Striped Alpaca Wrist Warmers

Materials:
"Misti" (100% alpaca, 55 yds / 50 m per 50 g) for wrist warmers. For the pink edging, I used "Faerytale" (100% alpaca, 191 yd / 175 m per 50 g); crochet hook suitable for yarn; lurex yarn for flowers, pretty mother-of-pearl buttons, needle and thread.

Instructions:
Note: Crochet the wrist warmers rather loosely so they'll be soft and stretchy.

1. Chain as many sts as needed to go around your wrist. I started with ch 23 with Misti and hook US size J-10 / 6 mm. I crocheted loosely throughout. Worked in sc throughout and turn each row with ch 1. Crochet 4 rows with one color and then change colors.

2. After 4 stripes, make a hole for the thumb as follows: when you get to the place for the thumbhole (I made 6 sc before the gap), ch 4, skip 4 sc in row below and then insert hook into 5th st for next sc. Sc across and turn with ch 1 and sc back as usual, including over the chain loop.

Edging
For the edging I used pink Faerytale and hook US size C-2 / 2.5 mm. Ch 3 and work 2 dc into first sc; next 3 dc into each sc across. Cut yarn and weave in tails.
   With RS facing RS, seam with matching sewing thread and small stitches. Turn wrist warmers RS out.

Flower
I used a lurex and glitter yarn and hook US size B-1.

1. Ch 4 and join into a ring with sl st.

2. Ch 6 and then 1 dc into ring. Work *ch 3, 1 dc around ring*. Rep from * to * until there are a total of 6 dc in ring.

3. Crochet flower petals as follows: into each chain loop around, work 1 sc, 1 hdc, 3 dc, 1 hdc, 1 sc.
   Sew a pretty little button at the center of the flower and then sew the flower securely to wrist warmer.

These alpaca
wrist warmers
are so soft and
lovely that
you might want
to wear them
all the time.

Lilac Mohair Shawl

Materials:
2 colors of mohair yarn (+ 1 for the flower), crochet
hook suitable for yarn, crocheted ball or make your own
and sew on (see how-to under Key Chain Balls), ribbon
for edging of shawl.

Instructions:
1. The crocheted netting can be a bit difficult with
uneven yarn. My scarf is very loose because I crocheted
with a thin yarn and a slightly larger hook. I usually work
rather loosely in any case. Swatch first to make sure you
get the results you want.

   Ch 20 (my scarf is 5 ¼ in / 13 cm wide) and turn with
1 dc, working dc into the 5th ch from the hook. *Ch 1,
skip 1 ch and work 1 dc into next st*; rep * to * across.
Turn all rows with ch 3.

2. Work all remaining rows as for pattern on row 1. My
scarf was 39 ½ in / 100 cm long.

Turquoise Mohair Yarn Flower
1. Ch 8 and join into a ring with sl st. Work as many sc
into ring as you can.

2. Ch 8 (approx) and then join chain loop with 1 st st
into a sc. Work a total of 6 petals, spacing them evenly
around. Now sc around each chain loop with enough sts
that the petals hold their shape. Securely attach flower
to scarf with small stitches.

3. Sew a round crocheted ball to the center of the
flower. I bought my ball but you can crochet one like it
by following the instructions for the key chain balls on
page 69.

4. Sew a pretty ribbon to each short end of the scarf.

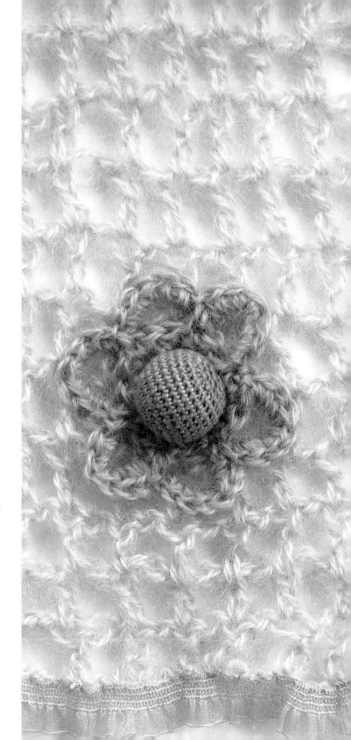

Long Net-Crocheted Scarf

Materials:
Pale color cotton yarn, crochet hook suitable for yarn, and a nice matching brooch.

Instructions:
1. Ch 23 (my scarf is 4 ¼ in / 11 cm wide) and then crochet 2 rows sc. Turn row with ch 5, 1 dc and insert hook into 2nd sc from end. *Ch 1, skip 1 ch of beginning chain and then work 1 dc into next st*; rep * to * across. Turn all rows with ch 3.

2. Crochet in net pattern until scarf is desired length (mine is 73 in / 185 cm long).

3. Work sc across the final 2 rows to match beginning. Cut yarn and weave in tails. Embellish scarf with a pretty brooch.

An elegant
and charming
pastel scarf.

SUMMER

Rose Hand Towel Edging

Materials:
A good quality hand towel, rose-colored smooth cotton yarn, crochet hook suitable for yarn I used hook US size D-3 / 3 mm, needle and matching thread for attaching edging to towel.

Instructions:
Ch as many sts as needed for one short edge of the towel. Turn.

1. Work 1 sc into 2nd chain from end of chain row, 1 sc into each of next 5 ch, * turn, ch 7, skip 5 sc, insert hook into the 6th sc and work 1 sc; turn, (6 sc around chain loop, ch 5, 6 sc around loop) in the 7-stitch loop, 1 sc into each of the next 7 ch from beg chain row; rep from * and end row with 1 sc in the last ch. Turn.

2. Ch 4, skip the 1st sc, *skip the next 6 sc, work (1 dc, ch 3, 1 sl st in the first of the 3 chain sts) 4 times in a 5 chain st loop, 1 dc in the same 5 chain st loop, skip 6 sc and work 1 tr centered between the 2 loops; rep from * across and end with a tr in chain st.

Steam press the edging before sewing it onto towel by hand with matching color thread and small, invisible stitches.

This rose-colored edging hangs like a row of little princess crowns on an otherwise very ordinary kitchen towel. It would make a very nice gift for someone who appreciates that little extra!

Large Flowered Pink Shawl

Materials:
Heavy wool yarn suitable for crochet hook US size J-10 / 6 mm and fine mohair yarn in matching color suitable for hook US size A / 2 mm, sewing needle and thread in matching color.

Instructions:
Flower
Ch 7 and join into a ring with sl st.

*1 sc around ring (do not work into the chain sts but work around ring), ch 4. Rep from * 6 more times and then work 1 sc around ring, ch 2 and 1 hdc into first sc.

Ch 5, 1 sc around chain loop. Rep this 6 more times, ch 2, 1 dc into hdc.

Ch 7, 1 sc around chain loop. Rep this 6 more times and then ch 3, 1 tr into dc.

Around each chain loop work: 1 sc, 1 hdc, 4 dc, ch 5 (make picot by joining last chain to first with sl st), 4 dc, 1 hdc, 1 sc. Rep into each loop. Cut yarn and weave in tails. Make a total of 10 flowers.

Join the flowers as shown in drawing. After joining all the large flowers, make the wheels.

Wheels between Flowers
With the finer mohair yarn and smaller crochet hook, ch 12 and join into a ring with sl st. Ch 6; 1 tr around ring, *ch 2, 1 tr around ring; rep from * until there are 12-15 tr total around ring, ch 2 and end by joining to beg of round with sl st. Do not cut yarn.

Joining Wheels
Ch 3 (continue with wheel just made), working as many sts as needed (depending on how thick the yarn is and how tightly you crochet), join ch loop to one of the thick flowers with 1 sc and then work in sc back along chain loop. Work 5-6 more sts around the wheel, ch 3 again as you join to a thick flower with 1 sc and then crochet back to wheel. Continue the same way and join the wheel with 5 or 6 spokes evenly spaced around the wheel

Fringe (optional): Holding both yarns together, cut 15 ¾ in / 40cm long strands for the fringe. Pull through the edge of the shawl, fold at center, and knot.

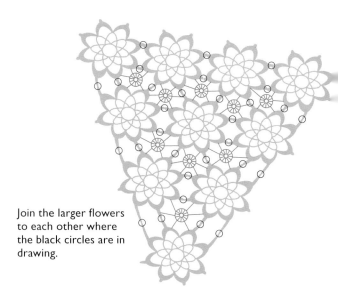

Join the larger flowers to each other where the black circles are in drawing.

Just right for a
summer party!

Round Potholders

Materials:
Small amounts of cotton fabric strips, large crochet hook – I used US size N-P/15 / 10 mm; finer cotton yarn for edging and smaller hook suitable for yarn.

Crocheting with fabric strips isn't difficult but it can be heavy work, so you'll need some muscle power! I usually hold the crochet hook with both hands to manage it. It is easier to crochet with thinner strips but then the potholders won't be as insulating. I used strips about 1 ¼ in / 3.5 cm wide for thick strong potholders.

Instructions:
1. With fabric strips and larger hook, ch 4 and join into a ring with sl st.

2. Work 2 or 3 sc into each ch st for a few rounds. After the first rnd, experiment to see how much to increase. If the potholder is bowl-shaped, you haven't increased enough; if it is loose and wavy, you added too many stitches.

3. Crochet around to desired size. My potholders are about 8 in / 20 cm in diameter.

4. End the last rnd with 3-5 sl sts for a rounded and smooth finishing.

Edging for the pink-white potholder with pale pink edge:
I used crochet hook US size G-6 / 4 mm.

1. Work sc around the potholder. You should work several sc into each stitch because of the difference between the yarn and fabric.

2. Continue as follows: *work 1 sc, 1 hdc, 4 dc, ch 4, join last ch with first with sl st, 4 dc, 1 hdc, 1 sc; rep from * around.

3. Hanging Loop: Ch 20 and join the cord securely to the potholder in same st as for beginning of loop. Turn and work sc around the loop. Cut yarn and weave in tail.

Edging for the Tweed Potholder:
For this potholder, I worked 2 rnds of sc around the edge. I made the hanging loop as above but spaced the loop ends further apart.

Colorful potholders to brighten up your kitchen!

Light Blue Knitted Triangular Shawl

Materials:
Fine fuzzy yarn, knitting needles US size 19 / 15 mm (so that the shawl will be very open); for the fringe: fabric with small printed designs matching the yarn (I used gingham and flower print fabrics); make sure the fabric won't unravel easily (= fabric that is woven well and evenly). Crochet hook suitable for yarn (approx US size D-3 / 3 mm).

Instructions:
The shawl is knitted in garter stitch = knit all rows.

1. With fuzzy yarn and larger needles, CO 3 sts. Inc 1 st at each side on every row (= k1f&b into first and last sts of row) until shawl is desired size. My shawl is 51 ¼ in / 130 cm wide at the top.

2. Bind off and weave in all tails. BO as follows: K2, *pass the right st over the left st on right needle. K1*; rep * to * across.

3. Crochet 2 rounds of sc all around the shawl so that the edge is strong and smooth.

4. Cut fabric into ribbons about 3/8 / 1 cm wide and 15 ¾ in / 40 cm long.

Note: Make sure the fabric is tightly woven. If it is too loose, the strips will unravel. Mix up the patterns. Thread and tie the strips into the edging of the shawl, spacing them evenly.

Decorative Circles for a Cardigan

I am a master at making spots on my light colored sweaters so here's my solution. Sew cute, decorative circles over the spots or add to a plain sweater to dress it up!

Materials:
Two colors of fine cotton embroidery thread and crochet hook US size A / 2 mm, sewing needle and matching thread.

Instructions:
Ch 6 and join into a ring with sl st. Ch 3, 1 dc around ring, *ch 1, 1 dc; rep from * around until circle is full and round. End with 1 sl st into first dc to join the circle. I made 8 dc into my circle.

Steam press circles on WS to flatten.

Use matching sewing thread to attach circles spread out over the sweater front.

Give your cardigan new life by adding decorative **circles!**

Pillow Flowers

Use these flowers to embellish clothing or accessories!

Materials:
Cotton yarn and crochet hook US size D-3 / 3 mm, matching sewing thread for attaching the flowers.

Instructions:

1. Ch 8 and join into a ring with sl st.

2. Ch 6, 1 dc around ring = 1 flower petal.

3. *Ch 3, 1 dc around ring* = 1 petal. Rep * to * 3 more times. The last petal ends with ch 3 and is joined with sl st to the last ch of the 1st dc. There should now be 6 petals around.

4. Into each ch loop around, work: 1 sc, 1 hdc, 3 dc, 1 hdc, 1 sc.

5. *Ch 5 and join with sl st to st between 2 petals; rep from * around.

6. Into each ch loop around, work: 1 sc, 1 hdc, 5 dc, 1 hdc, 1 sc.

7. *Ch 7 and join with sl st to st between 2 petals of the 2nd layer of petals; rep from * around.

8. Into each ch loop around, work: 1 sc, 1 hdc, 7 dc, 1 hdc, 1 sc.

9. Cut yarn and weave in tails. Sew flowers onto pillow.

Dress up your plain pillows by adding colorful flowers using leftover yarn!

Cable-Knit Pink Bag

If you haven't knitted before, it is probably not a good idea to begin with a double cable pattern. However, I'm not that great of a knitter and I managed this quite well. Why not try out cable knitting with this small piece. The rest of the bag is worked in single crochet and it's really easy.

Materials:
4 shades of pink yarn for the cable knitting (I used 4 different types of wool yarn in various pink tones), knitting needles US size 13 / 9 mm; cable needle, heavy crochet yarn for the rest of the bag, crochet hook US size J-10 / 6 mm, smooth wooden handle, sewing needle and thread.

Instructions:
I held 4 strands of wool yarn in various tones of pink together for the knitting. The knitting goes so much faster when you work with big yarn!

1. With US size 13 / 9 mm ndls, CO 18 sts. Row 1 (RS): P3, k12, p3. Row 2: K3, p12, k3.

2. The first cable row begins with p3. Now place the next 3 sts on a cable ndl behind work, k3 and then k3 from cn; place the next 3 sts on cn in front of work, k3, k3 from cn; end row with p3.

3. Next row (WS): K3, p12, k3; turn and, on RS: P3, k12, p3. Work a total of 5 rows between cable rows.

4. Repeat steps 2 and 3 until piece is about 11 ¾ in / 30 cm long. BO as follows: K2, *pass the right st over the left st on right needle, k1*; rep * to * across. Cut yarn and weave in tails.

Crochet the rest of the bag
1. Work in sc along long side of knitted cable. Turn each row with ch 1.

2. Work back and forth in sc until crochet section is 13 in / 33 cm long and then crochet to other side of knitted cable.

3. Turn bag inside out and securely seam lower edge using doubled strand of sewing thread. Turn bag right side out.

4. Attach handles by folding the knit fabric over the handle edge and sewing firmly with small stitches. If the handles have holes, sew through them to attach to bag.

The
cable-
knit
design
makes
this bag
irresist-
ible.

Silver Necklace

Materials:
Silver lurex yarn, Knitting Nancy (cord knitter) (available from craft shops), sewing needle and thread.

Instructions:
Read the instructions for your cord knitter and "knit" cord by looping around pins. I made my silver necklace with one color only but, of course, you could blend in the silver lurex yarn for a multi-colored necklace.

Make pin cushions with your leftover yarns. Use your imagination and play with colors and patterns. Anything goes!

Fantasy Flower

Materials:
Fine cotton yarn, crochet hook suitable for yarn (I used US size A / 2 mm), matching sewing thread and needle.

Instructions:
1. Make a flat circle: Ch 4 and join into a ring with sl st.

2. Inc by working 2 sc into each of the sts in row below. When circle is approx ¾ in / 2 cm in diameter, end with about 3 sl sts for an even finishing to the circle. Sew circle to desired spot on sweater.

3. Now make the petals. Long petal: Ch 16; turn and sc into each ch. At the end of the row, do not turn. Instead sc into the other side of the beginning chain sts. End row with 2 sl sts.

Work subsequent petals the same way, varying the number of ch sts as desired.

Make the petals various lengths. When you attach them, turn them slightly so that they look livelier and swing this way and that.

Sew the petals on as you work so that you can decide whether the next one should be long or short.

Felted Wool Bracelet

Materials:
Heavy wool yarn, crochet hook US size J-10 / 6 mm, decorative beads, sewing needle and thread.

Instructions:
1. Chain a cord long enough to go around your wrist plus an inch or so / a few cm because the band will shrink when felted.

2. Sc into each chain; do not turn at end of row. Sc into lower loops of chain so the band looks the same on each side. I finished my bracelet at this point because I used heavy yarn (two tweed yarns and two single color ones). You may wish to crochet more rows.

3. Place bracelet into a nylon net washing bag and machine-wash at 140°F / 60°C with a regular load of clothes. Make sure the clothes are the same color as the bracelet so they won't be affected by bleeding.

4. When the bracelet comes out of the washer it should be felted, hard and compact. Let bracelet dry completely and then decorate with beads as you like!

Heavy wool yarn, a crochet hook, some beads, a needle and thread – all you need for making beautiful bracelets.

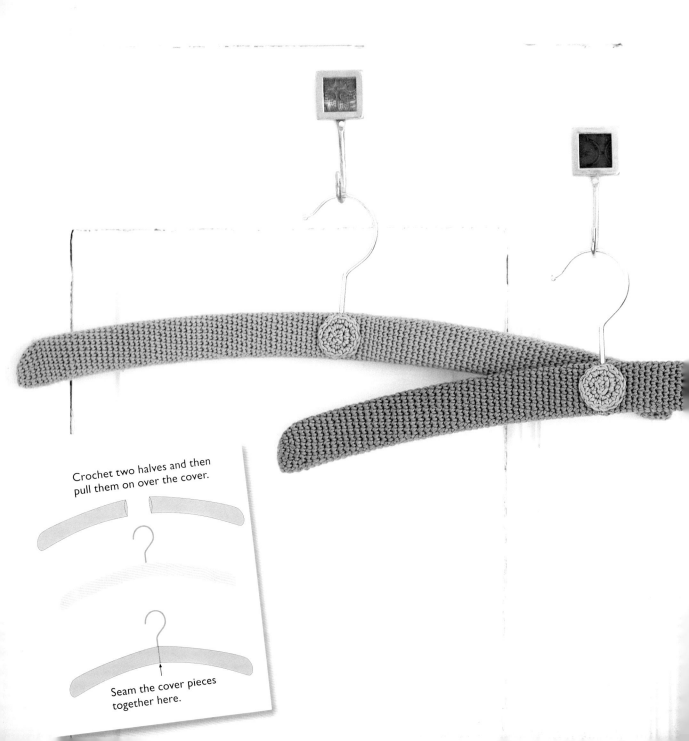

Crochet two halves and then pull them on over the cover.

Seam the cover pieces together here.

Lilac Coat Hangers

Materials:
Cotton yarn and crochet hook US size A / 2 mm or size suitable for your yarn, sewing needle and matching thread, slightly curved coat hangers.

Instructions:
1. Ch 5 and join into a ring with sl st.

2. Now work around in sc. On the first few rnds, work 2 sc into each ch/st to form a circle. When the circle is wide enough to go around the coat hanger, continue around in sc, without any further increases. After a few rounds, the piece should be shaped like a bowl. If it isn't, decrease a few stitches evenly spaced around.

Pull the piece over the coat hanger to make sure it fits. Make sure that your stitch count remains consistent throughout so that the cover doesn't get larger or smaller!

3. Crochet as many rounds as needed to reach the middle of the hanger. Put piece aside and make another the same way. Place pieces on each side of hanger. Sew together with matching thread and very small stitches. Make sure seam is secure!

Circles
1. Crochet a flat circle and place it at the center front of the hanger cover if you like. Make circle as follows: Ch 4 and join into a ring with sl st.

2. Work in sc, with 2 sc into each st of rnd below. When circle is desired size, end with 3-4 sl st for an even and smooth finishing to the circle.

3. Sew circle to coat hanger cover.

Round Pins for a Bag

Materials:
Large buttons – best in an assortment of sizes, various types of yarn, crochet hook suitable for yarn, sewing needle and thread, smooth mother-of-pearl button and fiber fill.

Instructions:
Crochet with small, tight stitches so that the button won't show through.

1. Crochet a flat circle to cover a button: ch 4 and join into a ring with sl st.

2. On the first 2-3 rnds, work 2 sc into each st around. Now you'll have to judge how many stitches/increases you need. Usually increasing into every other stitch works well. When the circle is large enough, end with 3-4 sl sts for a smooth finishing to the circle. Make the circle about ¼ in / .5 cm wider than the button so that you have an edge to fold over around the button. Stuff with a bit of fiber fill (or yarn in the same color) so that the brooch is soft and convex. Stitch together with sewing thread – see drawing.

3. Securely sew the brooch to the bag or sew a large safety pin to the brooch and pin to bag.

On one of the pins, I sewed a small mother-of-pearl button. Another brooch is made with fabric. I made it the same way as for the crocheted cover, using a small piece of fabric instead.

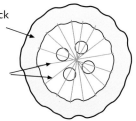

Crocheted edge folded over to back of button.

Stitches joining the cover to hold it in place securely.

Cover buttons in various sizes – an easy way to decorate your bag !

Bag Made from a Scarf

Materials:
A thick tweed yarn with two brown tones, three pink tones and white + some glitter yarn. Crochet hook suitable for yarn (I used US size J-10 / 6 mm), sewing needle and thread.

Instructions:
1. Ch as many stitches as you want for the width of your bag. My bag is 8 in / 20 cm wide.

2. Work back and forth in sc and turn each row with ch 1.

3. After my bag was 16 ½ in / 42 cm long, I cut the yarn and wove in the tails.

4. Fold the piece at the center of the length and, with RS facing RS, seam with a doubled strand of thread. Turn right side out.

5. Handle: I crocheted a wide handle that I folded in half and seamed so it would be very strong. Ch as many sts as needed for the length of the handle – mine is 9 ¾ in / 25 cm long. I made my handle 3 ¼ in / 8 cm wide so, folded, it is about 1 ½ in / 4 cm wide. Seam the handle and turn right side out. Sew handle securely to corners of bag.

Flower
Materials:
Pink lurex yarn with glitter and crochet hook US size 0-1 / 1-2 mm, matching thread to sew on flower.

Instructions:
1. Ch 8 and join into a ring with sl st.

2. Ch 6, 1 dc around ring = 1st flower petal.

3. Ch 3, 1 dc around ring = 2nd flower petal. Rep this step 3 more times. Make the last petal with ch 3, join last st to 1st dc. You should have 6 petals around.

4. Into each chain loop, work: 1 sc, 1 hdc, 3 dc, 1 hdc, 1 sc = 6 petals.

5. *Ch 5 and join with sl st to st between 2 petals; rep from * around.

6. Into each ch loop around, work: 1 sc, 1 hdc, 5 dc, 1 hdc, 1 sc.

7. *Ch 7 and join with sl st to st between 2 petals of the 2nd layer of petals; rep from * around.

8. Into each ch loop around, work: 1 sc, 1 hdc, 7 dc, 1 hdc, 1 sc.

9. Cut yarn and weave in tails. Sew flower where you like it on bag.

Sometimes it is hard to find exactly the right yarn for a project. What about checking a clothing store or thrift shop? You'll undoubtedly find a wide selection of scarves made from heavy and fine yarns. This bag is made with a cheap scarf that I ripped out so I could crochet with the yarn.

Key Ring Balls

Materials:
Various types of yarn and hook suitable for yarn, stuffing for balls (for example, the same yarn, fiber fill or a marble), a key ring, sewing needle and matching thread.

Instructions:
Note: The balls must be crocheted tightly so that the stuffing doesn't fall out.

1. Ch 4 and join into a ring with sl st.

2. Work 6 sc around ring = not into the chain st but around the chain loop.

3. Inc by working 2 sc into each st of rnd below = 12 sc around.

4. Work 3 rnds with 1 sc into each st of rnd below.

5. Stuff the ball with fabric (color matching yarn) or the same yarn you crocheted with. You could also stuff the ball with fiber fill but it is almost always white and could be visible through the crochet. If you don't crochet tightly enough, the fiber fill might poke out between the stitches. If you want a heavier ball, put a marble into it.

6. Dec by working 1 sc into every other st around until ball is closed. Make sure that you crochet tightly enough that there are no holes between the stitches. Crochet the ball top together and then make a chain a couple of inches / a few cm long so you can attach the ball to the key ring. I simply knotted the chain cords together and then sewed the knot with tiny stitches so it wouldn't loosen. When everything was secured well, I cut the yarn and wove the tails in.

Where are my keys? Now it will be easier to find them in your bag.

Coasters

Materials:
Fine smooth embroidery yarn, crochet hook
US size 10 / 1 mm.
You can change colors as much as you want.

Instructions:
1. Ch 5 and join into ring with sl st.

2. Ch 3 (= 1 dc), *1 dc, ch 1; rep from * until there are a total of 8 dc in ring. Join last ch to the top of the ch 3 at beg of rnd with sl st.

3. Ch 5, *1 dc around the chain between the dc of previous rnd, ch 2, 1 dc between the dc of previous rnd, ch 2; rep from * until there are 16 dc around. Join last ch to top of first dc with sl st.

4. Change colors if you want. Ch 5, *1 dc between the dc of previous rnd (into chain loop) and ch 2 between all dc.* If you are crocheting tightly, you might need 3 chain sts instead of 2 between each dc – test and decide. Rep * to * until there are 16 dc around. Join the last 2 ch to the 1st dc with sl st.

5. Ch 5 (= 1st dc), *1 dc around chain loop, ch 2, 1 dc around chain loop, ch 2, 1 dc around same chain loop as previous dc* = 2 dc into the same loop. Rep * to * until there are a total of 24 dc around. Join last 2 ch with the 1st dc with sl st.

6. Ch 5 (= 1 dc) and then work 1 dc into every chain loop of previous rnd; alternate ch 2 and ch 3 between each dc. Join the last 2 ch with sl st to 1 st dc of rnd. Cut yarn and weave in all tails.

7. Work 1 or 2 rnds sc around the coaster for a firmer edge. Steam press coaster on WS so it will be flat and smooth.

These attractive coasters go well with the Moroccan tea glasses.

AUTUMN

Triangular Shawl

Materials:

Three colors of "Fine Alpaca" (100% alpaca, 182 yds / 167 m per 50 g), crochet hook US size G-6 / 4 mm.

Instructions:

1. Ch as many stitches as you want for top of shawl. My shawl is 53 ¼ in / 135 cm across. If there are a few too many stitches on the first shell row, you can unravel the extra chain sts.

Row 1: Turn and work 1 dc in the 5th ch from hook, *ch 2, skip 5 ch, and, into the 6th ch, work 1 dc, ch 2, 1 dc. Rep from *. End row with 1 dc, ch 2, 1 dc into last ch so that a triangle is shaped when the piece is turned upside down. Turn at end of row.

Row 2: Ch 2, *8 dc around the chain-2 loop between the 2 dc of previous row =insert hook under loop and not into the ch stitches), skip next loop; rep from * across. Turn.

Row 3: Sl st over to the 4th or 5th dc (the centermost stitch of shell), ch 4, 1 dc into the same st, *ch 2, 1 dc into the 5th dc of next group of dc, ch 2, 1 dc into the same stitch as previous dc; rep from * across. Turn.

Now rep rows 2 and 3.

For a triangular shawl, I worked 2 rows of the shell pattern for the same length across and then I narrowed the shawl by slip stitching back for a half shell. On the shell (at the center of shell on previous row) I worked ch 4 as the 1st dc of that row.

Change colors as you like or work shawl in one color.

When the shawl is complete, work 3 rows of sc across the top to stabilize the edge. Cut yarn and weave in all tails.

Shell Pattern Edging for a Skirt

Materials:
Same as for shawl.

Instructions:
I had a knit skirt that I could crochet directly into using a very fine hook for the sc row. Begin by working sc around the skirt edge. If you don't have a knit skirt, you can crochet a strip of the shell pattern and sew it by hand onto the skirt hem. After the sc row, work around in the shell pattern above or turn at the end of every row (sl st 4-5 sts and then ch 4); seam and sew on by hand if necessary.

Gray-green Jewelry Bag

Materials:
"Mirasol" (100% alpaca, 137 yds / 125 m per 50 g) (work with two strands held together and hook US size G-6 / 4 mm) and fuzzy "Nanuk" (100% alpaca, 44 yds / 40 m per 50 g) (worked with a single strand and hook US G-6 / 4 mm); small amounts for balls and a zipper in matching color.

Instructions:
For my bag, I contrasted a bright green yarn with gray fuzzy alpaca. The fuzzy alpaca yarn looks like felted stripes.

1. Ch 35 (for a wider bag, chain a few more sts); turn and continue in sc. I worked 5 rows of green (not counting the chain row at beginning) and then changed to gray for 1 row.

2. Rep the green and gray stripe sequence until piece is 15 ¾ in / 40 cm long. The bag will be folded in half and then be about 8 in / 20 cm long.

3. Open the zipper and pin it into place on inside of bag; baste and then machine-stitch.

Small balls – crocheted with fine yarn and hook US size B-1 / 2.5 mm.

Note: The balls must be crocheted tightly so the stuffing doesn't poke out.

1. Ch 4 and join into a ring with sl st.

2. Work 6 sc around ring (= do not work into the chain sts but around them).

3. Work 2 sc into each sc of rnd below = 12 sc total.

4. Work 3 rnds of sc with 1 sc into each st.

5. Stuff the ball (in matching fabric or the same yarn as crocheted with). You could also stuff the balls with fiber fill but it is almost always white and will show through.

6. Work 1 sc into every other st of previous rnd until ball is finished. Crochet tightly so there are no holes between stitches. Crochet the top opening together and then ch a couple of inches / a few cm so you can attach the balls to the zipper loop.

An assortment of yarns makes a great contrast. Try it!

Rose-Champagne Knitted Wrist Warmers

Materials:
For my pair, I used two handspun yarns that were uneven in thickness; one yarn shifted colors from champagne to rose pink. This yarn was expensive but lovely to knit with. Knitting needles US size 6 / 4mm. Sewing needle and matching thread.

Instructions:
1. CO 24 sts rather loosely (the cast-on row has to be elastic so you can get the wrist warmers over your hands). Work 6 rows in k2/p2 ribbing.

Note: For my hand size and the yarn I used, 24 sts were sufficient. Work a swatch first to make sure that the yarn and number of stitches make a piece to fit you.

2. Now change yarn and work 20 rows in stockinette.

3. Finish as for beginning with 6 rows k2/p2 ribbing.

4. BO loosely in ribbing; cut yarn and weave in tails neatly on WS.

5. With RS facing RS, seam wrist warmers with small stitches. You can use the same yarn you knitted with or a doubled strand of matching sewing thread so the seam line won't be visible.

Knitted Pink Mohair Scarf

Materials:
Very fuzzy mohair yarn and knitting needles
US size 13 / 9 mm.

Instructions:
1. CO 36 sts with US 13 / 9 mm ndls. Of
course, you can change the number of sts for
the width of scarf you want or the yarn you
have chosen.

2. Work in k1/p1 ribbing throughout.

3. Work until scarf is desired length. Mine is
59 in / 150 cm long.

4. BO as follows: K2, *pass the right st over
the left st on right needle, k1*; rep * to *
across. Cut yarn and weave in tails on WS.

A cozy and attractive shawl to sling over your shoulders when the days start getting shorter and the evenings cooler.

Purple Triangular Shawl

Materials:
Medium weight yarn and crochet hook suitable for yarn, small amount of mohair in contrasting color, brooch to secure shawl.

Instructions:
1. The shawl is crocheted from the top (widest) down. Ch as many sts as needed for desired width. My shawl is 43 ¼ in / 110 cm across.

2. Turn, with yarn over hook, insert hook into 5th ch from hook and work 1 dc, ch 1, skip 1 st, and dc into next st. Rep (ch 1, skip 1, 1 dc) across.

3. Turn but do not ch; instead sl st to next dc. When you are at the 1st dc of the previous row, work as follows: ch 5, yarn over hook, insert hook into next dc and complete dc + ch 1. On the next to last dc, turn and sl st to next dc. See drawing for shaping. Continue until shawl reaches tip.

4. When the shawl has been crocheted, the edges will look like stair steps. With shawl body yarn, work 1 row of sc around the whole shawl. If you want a firmer edging, work 2 rnds sc.

5. With fuzzy mohair yarn in contrasting color, work 1 rnd sc around. Cut yarn and weave in all tails on WS.

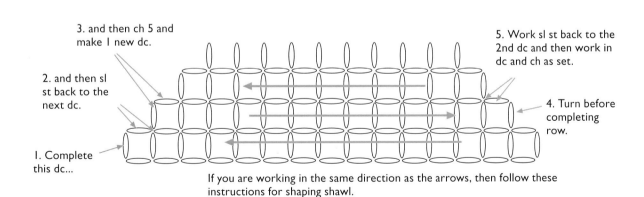

3. and then ch 5 and make 1 new dc.

2. and then sl st back to the next dc.

1. Complete this dc...

5. Work sl st back to the 2nd dc and then work in dc and ch as set.

4. Turn before completing row.

If you are working in the same direction as the arrows, then follow these instructions for shaping shawl.

Gray Necklace with Glass Hearts

Materials:
Fine, smooth crochet yarn, heart-shaped glass beads with large holes, crochet hook US size 1-2 / 2 mm

Instructions:

1. Ch as many stitches as needed for desired length; my necklace is about 39 ½ in / 1 meter long.

2. Turn and work 1 dc into each chain across.

3. Pull the yarn tails through the glass hearts and tie a little knot behind the heart if needed. Trim all yarn ends.

You can make this pretty necklace as fast as 1-2-3!

Brooch with Lurex Petals

Materials:
Rug wool or cotton yarn and lurex yarn in matching colors for the flower petals, crochet hook suitable for yarn, a large button or card stock, sewing needle and matching thread.

Instructions:
Crochet tightly so the button won't show through.

1. Make a flat circle to sew over a button as follows: ch 4 and join into a ring with sl st.

2. Work 2 sc into each of the sts of row below for the first 2-3 rnds. Now decide how many increases are needed. Usually an inc in every other st works well. When the circle is desired size, end with 3-4 sl sts for a smooth finishing. Make the circle about 3/8 in / .5 cm larger than the button. Secure circle over button (see drawing).

3. Now change to lurex yarn. Insert hook into the crocheted button through a sc near the edge and then ch 6 and 1 sl st along the button edge so that it becomes a chain st loop = 1st petal; rep around until there are 8 petals total.

Note: Make sure the chain st loops are all the same length around.

4. Around each chain st loop work: 1 sc, 1 hdc, 6 dc, 1 hdc, 1 sc.
 Cut yarn and weave in tails. Sew brooch to a hat.

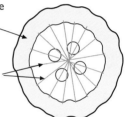

The crocheted edge is folded over the button on WS.

Stitch as shown to hold the button securely within the crocheted circle.

Scarf Instructions:
With fuzzy mohair yarn and knitting ndls US size 10 / 6 mm, CO approx 36 sts. Work back and forth in k2/p2 ribbing for 2 in / 5 cm. Change to another yarn and work in stockinette until scarf is desired length. Change back to the fuzzy mohair and work in k2/p2 ribbing for 2 in / 5 cm. BO loosely as follows: K2, *pass the right st over the left st on right needle. K1*; rep * to * across.

Shell-Pattern Scarf with Long Fringe

Materials:
Heavy pretty alpaca yarn "Misti" (100% alpaca, 55 yds / 50 m per 50 g), crochet hook US size J-10 / 6 mm. Small amounts of several turquoise shade yarns (I used 5 different shades and also some mohair for a more exciting effect).

Instructions:
This scarf is crocheted sideways; I worked a total of 8 rows.

1. For my 55 in / 140 cm long scarf, I began with ch 130. Turn, work 1 dc and then insert hook into the 4th ch from end. * In the next ch, work 2 dc; ‡ 1 ch, 2 dc, with yarn over hook, insert hook into the next beginning ch, pull yarn through, yarn around hook, and bring through 2 loops, yarn around hook, skip 3 ch sts, insert hook into the 4th ch and pull yarn through, yarn around hook, pull through 2 loops, yarn around hook and pull through last 2 loops ‡*. Rep from * to * across but end with the stitches between ‡ symbols so the edge will be straight.

2. Work remainder of scarf as follows: Ch 3, 1 dc into last st before chain hole between the 4 dc (see drawing),* make 1 group with 2 dc, ch 1, 2 dc around chain loop. ‡ Yarn around hook, and insert hook into the next st, pull yarn through, yarn around hook and pull through the 2 loops, yarn around hook, skip 3 sts, insert hook into the last st before the chain loop, pull yarn through, yarn around hook, pull through 2 loops, rep yarn through 2 loops 2 times until you have only 1 st on hook ‡*. Rep from * to * across. End all rows with the instructions between ‡ symbols. Begin every row with ch 3.

3. Fringe: Cut 15 ¾ in / 40 cm long strands of alpaca and other yarns and mix strands as desired for fringe. Pull the strands through short ends of scarf and knot each bundle to secure. Make sure the strands are even and smooth.

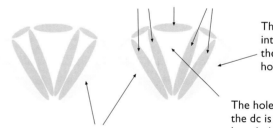

The pink lines show: 2 dc, 1 ch, 2 dc

This dc is worked into the st before the "chain loop hole"

The hole between the dc is a "chain loop hole"

These 2 "dc" are worked as follows: Yarn around hook, insert hook into st or chain, bring yarn through, yarn around hook, and bring through 2 loops, yarn around hook, skip 3 sts, insert hook into the 4th st (= the last st before the chain st opening), bring yarn through, yarn around hook, bring through 2 loops, and continue with yarn around hook and through 2 loops until 1 loop remains on hook.

Narrow Bracelets

Materials:
Metallic embroidery thread in two shades of turquoise, silver lurex yarn, black, medium pink, cerise, and fuzzy black yarn, crochet hook US size 1-2 / 2 mm, sewing needle and matching thread for seaming. The lurex yarn has metallic threads that glitter and shine!

Instructions:
Turquoise bracelet:
1. With one shade of turquoise metallic yarn, ch as many sts as needed to fit around your hand. Join into a ring with sl st. Work 1 round sc and then cut yarn; weave in tails on WS.

2. Attach the other shade of turquoise metallic yarn and work 5 sc across. Ch 3 and join the ch to last sc worked with sl st for a "picot." Work 5 sc and then another picot. Repeat around. Cut yarn.

3. Rep step 2 on the other side of the bracelet.

Silver bracelet with black lurex edging:
1. With silver lurex yarn, ch as many sts as needed to fit around your hand. Work 1 row in sc and then work around the corner and edge to the other side of beginning chain and sc across. Cut yarn and weave in tails. Seam bracelet.

2. With black lurex yarn, work in sc around each side of the bracelet. Cut yarn and weave in tails.

Black fuzzy bracelet with black lurex edging:
1. With fuzzy black yarn, ch as many sts as needed to go around your hand. Turn and work 1 row with sc and then sc around corner, edge, and other side of beginning chain. Cut yarn and weave in tails.

2. With black lurex yarn, sc around both sides of the bracelet. Cut yarns and weave in ends.

Granny Square Bracelet:
Use an assortment of lurex yarns for a granny square bracelet.
   Make square as follows:

1. Ch 5 and join into a ring with sl st.

2. Ch 3, 2 dc around ring (catching yarn tail at the same time) = the first 2 dc/the first dc group, ch 2, 3 dc around ring, ch 2, 3 dc around ring, ch 2, 3 dc around ring and ch 2. Join last ch with 2 sl st to top of the first dc group. Cut yarn.
   Make as many squares as needed for the bracelet to go around your hand. Seam the blocks together with very small stitches and doubled sewing thread.

Pretty metallic bracelets

Granny Square Hat

Materials:
Small amounts of wool yarn, crochet hook suitable for yarn – I used hook US size D-3 / 3 mm, sewing needle and matching thread.

Instructions:
1. First round of the square: Ch 3 with first color and join into a ring with sl st. Ch 3, 2 dc around ring (catching yarn tail at the same time) = the first 3 dc/the 1st dc group, ch 2, 3 dc around ring, ch 2, 3 dc around ring, ch 2, 3 dc around ring and ch 2; join the last ch with 1 sl st at the top of the 1st dc group. Cut yarn. See drawing on p. 99 for how to make squares.

2. Second round of the square:
Change to color 2 and begin at a corner. Ch 3, 2 dc = 1st dc group, ch 2, *3 dc, ch 2, 3 dc* (the sts inside the asterisks are the corner chain loop), ch 2, * 3 dc, ch 2, 3 dc* = corner chain st loop, ch 2, *3 dc, ch 2, 3 dc* = in corner chain st loop, ch 2, 3 dc, ch 2

and join last ch to 1st dc with sl st. Cut yarn.

3. 3rd and final rnd of the square: With color 3, begin at a corner ch loop with ch 3, 2 dc (= 1st dc group). Ch 2, 3 dc in next chain loop, ch 2, *3 dc, ch 2, 3 dc* = corner chain loop. Ch 2, 3 dc in next chain loop, ch 2, *3 dc, ch 2, 3 dc* = into corner chain loop. Ch 2, 3 dc in next chain loop, ch 2,* 3 dc, ch 2, 3 dc* = in corner chain loop. Ch 2, 3 dc in next chain loop, ch 2, and 3 dc into last corner chain loop. Ch 2 and join last ch with sl st to 1st dc group. Cut yarn and weave in tails.

Now the first granny square is complete!

Tip: If the chain loops are too short when made with ch 2, then try ch 3 between each dc group. Make sure, though, that the square doesn't get wavy.

4. Make as many squares as needed to go around head (my hat has 7 squares). With doubled thread in matching color, seam the squares together. Cut thread.

5. Now work rounds of sc along lower edge of squares. Make as many rows as needed to cover the ears and back neck. My brim was 1 ½ in / 4 cm long.

6. Work in sc for about 1 ½ / 4 cm along top edge of granny squares for the crown. On my hat the crown is 5 ¼ in / 13 cm long.

7. Begin shaping as follows:

Rnd 1: Dec 6 sts evenly spaced around.

Rnd 2: Sc around.

Rnd 3: Dec 6 sts evenly spaced around.

Rnds 4 and 5: Sc around.

Rnd 6: Dec 6 sts evenly spaced around.

Rnds 7 and 8: Sc around.

Try on hat. If the hat is too tight, take out a few rows and then make fewer decreases. If the hat is too loose, make more decreases on each dec rnd.

Rnd 9: Dec 6 sts evenly spaced around.

Rnds 10 and 11: Sc around.

Rnd 12: Dec 6 sts evenly spaced around.

Rnds 13 and 14: Sc around.

Rnds 15 and 16: Dec 6 sts evenly spaced around.

Remainder of hat: Dec on every 4th st. On the final dec rnd, dec on every other st and then you can crochet the hole at top together. Sew the rest of the hole together. Cut yarn and weave in tail neatly on WS.

Alpaca Block Throw

Materials:

5 colors of "Fine Alpaca" (100% alpaca, 182 yds / 167 m per 50 g), crochet hook US size G-6 / 4 mm (I made my blanket with 2 strands of yarn held together – if you crochet with a single strand, you'll need a smaller size hook).

Instructions:

1. Ch 20; yarn around hook and turn. Insert hook into the 4th ch and then dc into each ch across. Turn with ch 2.

2. Work back and forth in dc until block is 5 ½ in / 14 cm long. (My blocks are 4 ¼ x 5 ½ in / 11 x 14 cm).

3. Make a total of 30 blocks the same way. See drawing showing the color arrangement. Cut yarn and weave in all ends on WS.

4. Crochet the blocks together as follows: Arrange the blocks in the order you'd like. Join blocks with a single strand of white yarn. With blocks WS facing WS, crochet them together.

Fold each block vertically with RS facing RS and crochet edges together. Make sure that your stitches are even so that the edges won't be jagged.

5. With two strands of white yarn held together, work in sc all around the outside. As you crochet the first rnd, catch all the loose ends to cover them so the back will look neat. End first rnd with ch 2. Rnd 2: Dc into each sc around, with 3-4 dc at each corner so corners will be square.

Color arrangement

Fold the blocks two and two against each other and crochet together along all short sides. Now crochet the next two blocks together.

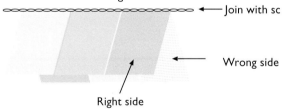

Join with sc

Wrong side

Right side

Turn the blanket the other way, with wrong sides facing each other, and crochet together along the long sides.

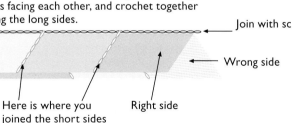

Join with sc

Wrong side

Right side

Here is where you joined the short sides

A lovely
pastel baby
blanket.
It's easy
to make
and a
guaranteed
winner
among the
gifts for
the little
one!

91

A sweet striped hat embellished with embroidery and buttons.

Beaded Turquoise Striped Hat

Materials:
Small amount of "Mirasol" (100% alpaca, 137 yds / 125 m per 50 g), crochet hook US size D-3 / 3 mm, smooth embroidery yarn, assorted colors and shapes of mother-of-pearl buttons, sewing needle and matching thread.

Instructions:
1. My baby hat is 18 ¼ in / 46 cm around but I crochet rather loosely – the hat was so elastic that it fit my 6-month old daughter. Ch as many sts as needed to go around the baby's head. Work straight up in sc to desired length to crown. The baby hat I made was not particularly long. It was more of a fall or spring hat rather than for winter. If you want a striped hat, space white stripes about 1 in / 2.5 cm apart. The stripe sequence on my hat is: 6 rnds turquoise, 2 rnds white.

2. For my hat, I worked in sc for 4 ¼ in / 11 cm. If you want the hat to cover the ears, work a few more rnds.

Crown shaping
Rnd 1: Dec 6 sts evenly spaced around.

Rnd 2: Sc around.

Rnd 3: Dec 6 sts evenly spaced around.

Rnds 4 and 5: Sc around.

Rnd 6: Dec 6 sts evenly spaced around.

Rnds 7 and 8: Sc around.

Try on hat. If the hat is too tight, take out a few rows and then make fewer decreases. If the hat is too loose, make more decreases on each dec rnd.

Rnd 9: Dec 6 sts evenly spaced around.

Rnds 10 and 11: Sc around.

Rnd 12: Dec 6 sts evenly spaced around.

Rnds 13 and 14: Sc around.

Rnds 15 and 16: Dec 6 sts evenly spaced around.

Remainder of hat: Dec on every 4th st. On the final dec rnd, dec on every other st and then you can crochet the hole at top together. Sew the rest of the hole together. Cut yarn and weave in neatly on WS.

Finish by working 1 or 2 rnds of sc with white around lower edge of hat so it will have a smooth edging. A chain st edging would probably be too loose and floppy.

Sew on the buttons (optional if for a small child) and then make French knots with the embroidery yarn. Use an assortment of yarns for the embroidered flowers. For my hat, I mixed matt thick wool yarn with smoother cotton yarns.

Little Slippers

These slippers will fit a one-year-old with somewhat chubby feet. You can adjust the size of the slippers by changing the sole so it fits the child who will get the slippers. Otherwise follow my pattern.

Materials:

Heathery yarn and crochet hook suitable for the yarn (I used hook US size G-6 / 4 mm for a medium thick yarn for slippers about 5 ¼ in / 13 cm long. Half-bleached white cotton yarn for edging and crochet hook US size D-3 / 3 mm, matching mother-of-pearl buttons, sewing needle and matching thread for sewing on buttons and a little extra: two small thin bits of suede leather to sew securely under the slippers so that the child won't slip. Wool socks and slippers are very slippery, so if you are making them for a child who is walking already, make sure that the soles are covered with a non-slippery fabric.

Instructions:

1. Make a cord of chain sts long enough for the baby's foot. Since it is important that the sole be sized correctly, fit the chain against the baby's foot. My son had feet 5 ½ in / 14 cm long so I made a chain 3 ½ in / 9 cm long and then worked in sc around and around until the sole was 5 ½ in / 14 cm long. See Illustration 1 on page 97. When working at the top and bottom of the piece, work 2 sc each into some of the sts so the sole will be flat instead of bowl-shaped. When sole is desired size, end with 3-4 sl sts for an even finishing.

Note: Make sure that you work the same number of rows on each side of the beginning chain so that the sole is the same width on both sides. Make the other sole the same way.

2. Now crochet the sides so that you have a little "boat." See Illustration 2 on page 97. Hold the sole with the inside facing you and work sc into the back loop (for the smoothest edge). Crochet the following rounds with sc into both loops. Make sure that you keep the stitch count consistent—don't increase! Work about 5 rnds in sc and then end with 3-4 sl sts on the final rnd. Make the other slipper the same way.

3. Sew the leather pieces to slipper soles.

4. Now you will make the toe for the slipper. Insert hook into a sc at the center of the "boat edge" (see Illustration 3 on page 97), ch straight over the "boat" and join to the other side (I made 9 ch but the number you'll need depends on your yarn and how tightly/loosely you crochet). The chain sts should be as long as the hole space so that they don't pull the slippers together or make them buckle. Crochet back and forth with sc and join the crochet with 1 or 2 sc at the "boat edges" each time you are finished with a row. Throughout, dec so that you follow the shape of the slipper. Continue the same way until 1 row before the toe. Now crochet the toe together and the row you are holding with (I had 5 sts to crochet together). Work into 1 loop only on both sides (see drawing).

See page 97 for pattern details

5. When you are finished, you'll have a little shoe. Try the slippers on the recipient. Weave in tails on WS and then make the other slipper the same way.

6. Work in sc around the cuff (see Illustration 5). I worked 2 rnds with sc and on the 3rd rnd, I decreased 5 sts evenly spaced around (so that the slipper sits better on the foot). If the baby has small ankles, you should dec more sts. Crochet straight up for about 3 ¼ in / 8 cm and then change color and yarn. I crocheted with white yarn for ¾ in / 2 cm. End the last rnd with 3 sl sts for a smooth finishing. Cut yarns and weave in tails. Fold leg/cuff at the middle and sew a pretty button at center front.

7. Make the other slipper the same way.

1. After making the chain, turn and work sc along one side of the chain; continue in sc around the other side of the chain and then around and around until the sole is the same size as child's foot.

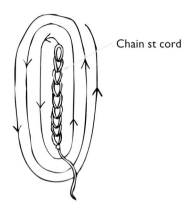

Chain st cord

2. Crochet around and straight up from the sole to make a "boat."

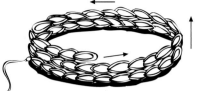

3. Work back and forth over the slipper: begin with chain st and then continue in sc; dec and adjust shaping so slipper will fit recipient.

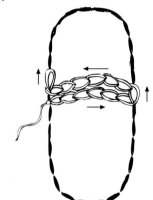

4. Crochet the slipper together at the front.

Toe of the "boat"

Crocheted section over foot/"boat"

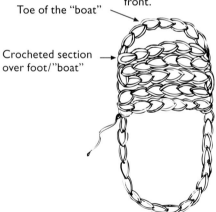

Toe of the "boat" Insert hook only through adjacent loops

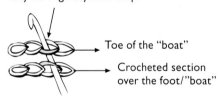

Toe of the "boat"

Crocheted section over the foot/"boat"

5. Crochet around the ankle and then continue straight up

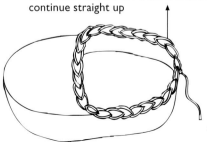

Granny Square Baby Blanket

Materials:

Small amounts of wool and cotton yarns in assorted colors. Make sure the yarns are the same size so that the squares will be equal-sized. Crochet hook US size D-3 / 3 mm, white cotton yarn for edging the squares and blanket, sewing needle and matching thread.

Instructions:

1. Center of square: With the first color, ch 5 and join into a ring with sl st. Ch 3, 2 dc around ring (catching the yarn end) = 3 dc/the first dc group. (Ch 2, 3 dc) 3 times, ch 2. Join last ch to first dc with sl st. Cut yarn. See drawings for details of crocheting the blocks.

2. Second round of square: Change color and begin in one corner. Ch 3, 2 dc = 1st dc group. *Ch 2, 3 dc, ch 2, 3 dc* = sts worked into corner ch loop. Work * to * 3 times and end with ch 2, 3 dc, ch 2 into same corner as 1st dc group; join last ch to top of first dc with sl st. Cut yarn.

3. Third round of square: Change color and begin in a corner. Ch 3, 2 dc = 1st dc group. *Ch 2, 3 dc into next ch 2 loop; ch 2, 3 dc, ch 2, 3 dc into corner chain loop; rep from * around, ending with ch 2, 3 dc, ch 2 into beginning corner; join last ch to top of first dc with sl st. Cut yarn.

4. Work the fourth round of square with white yarn. Work as for step 3 with ch 2, 3 dc into each ch 2 loop between corners and ch 2, 3 dc, ch 2, 3 dc into each corner. Join as for previous rnds and cut yarn.

Now the first granny square is complete! For my baby blanket, I made a total of 42 squares.

Tip: If the ch 2 loops are too short between the dc groups, try ch 3 between each dc group. Make sure, though, that the blanket doesn't get wavy.

5. With a doubled strand of white sewing thread and WS facing WS sew the blocks together securely. After joining all the blocks, crochet 3 or more rounds of 3 dc, ch 2 groups, with 3 dc, ch 2, 3 dc in each corner. Cut yarn and weave in ends.

The first square

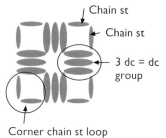

Chain st

Chain st

3 dc = dc group

Corner chain st loop

The second square (pale pink)

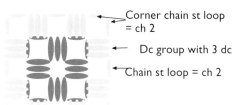

Corner chain st loop = ch 2

Dc group with 3 dc

Chain st loop = ch 2

The third square (green)

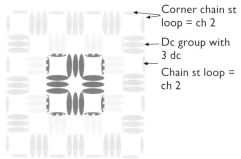

Corner chain st loop = ch 2

Dc group with 3 dc

Chain st loop = ch 2

99

Teething Ring

Materials:

Various colors of Mercerized cotton yarn (I used 8 colors), crochet hook suitable for yarn, fiber fill, sewing needle and matching thread to sew ring together.

Instructions:

1. I made a rectangle that I seamed to form a sausage shape. I filled it with fiber fill and then sewed the ends to each other. You could crochet a sausage by working around and around and then you won't have to seam the long edges.

For a rectangle, ch 11, turn and work back and forth in sc. Every few rows, change colors. It is very important that you crochet tight little stitches so that the stuffing doesn't come out through the holes at the sides.

2. When the rectangle is about 11 in / 28 cm long, cut yarn and weave in tail.

3. Sew the piece into a sausage shape: fold the piece lengthwise and join long edges with small stitches (be very precise); cut yarn. Turn "sausage" right side out and fill.

4. Sew the ends to each other to form a ring. Make sure that the sewing is very secure to that the piece can't open up.

Children's Striped Leg Warmers

Materials:
Various colors of cotton yarn (some tweedy cotton yarn will make the leg warmers especially pretty), crochet hook suitable for yarn, sewing needle and matching thread.

Instructions:
1. Chain as many sts as needed to go around foot. Turn and insert hook into 4th ch and then dc across rem chain sts. Continue working back and forth in dc; turn each row with ch 2.

2. Change colors as desired. I worked 2 rows with some colors and only 1 row with others.

3. Weave in all ends on WS. With a doubled strand of sewing thread and RS facing RS, seam leg warmers and then turn right side out.

Little girls love to get decked out with stylish accessories!

Polka Dot Sweater

Size:
approx 2 years

Materials:
3 colors of "Babysilk" (80% baby alpaca, 20% silk, 145 yds / 133 m per 50 g), crochet hook US size C / 2.5 mm.

PLEASE READ BEFORE YOU START!

Before crocheting a garment, find a similar one to measure from. If you want to crochet a sweater, get a sweater that fits the child. At every step of the process, check the crochet work against the finished sweater. Lay the crochet pieces against the finished garment so that you can verify that the armholes, neck, length, width, etc always match. If you continually compare the work in progress with the finished piece, you can be sure there won't be any big problems and you'll avoid a lot of frustration!

I used a rather fine yarn for this sweater and crocheted somewhat loosely so it is difficult to give you precise measurements. If you use a thicker yarn, the stitch count will be totally different.

If you want to crochet this sweater in a smaller or larger size, it's not hard to make the adjustments. You can follow my general instructions and increase/decrease as necessary to match the finished garment that fits the intended recipient.

Instructions:
Back

1. Chain as many stitches as necessary for desired width of the sweater. My sweater is 11 ¾ in / 30 cm wide at the lower edge.

2. Work 1 dc into each chain st across. Turn every row with ch 2 (these 2 ch = the first dc of the next row. On the first row after the chain, with yarn over hook, insert hook into 3rd ch from hook and complete a dc).

3. Continue working back and forth in double crochet to desired length to armholes. I crocheted 8 in / 20 cm to the underarm. Measure a sweater that fits the child so you'll know when to begin increasing for the sleeves.

4. Sleeve shaping: Inc 1 dc at each side = work 2 dc into 1 dc of previous row instead of only 1. Increase the same way on both sides a total of 3 times. See drawing.

5. Chain as many stitches as necessary for sleeve length. The sleeves on my sweater are 5 ¼ in / 13 cm long so I chained 30 sts at each side. Check the original sweater to see how long the sleeves should be. I made the sleeves for my sweater somewhat shorter than full length because they are rather wide and could easily land in the food when the child is eating!

On one sleeve, add 2 ch (= 1st dc). On my sweater, there are 30 chain sts on one sleeve and 32 chain sts on the other. Continue in double crochet.

6. When sleeve is 4 ¼ in / 10.5 cm long (measure against original sweater again), begin neck shaping. I skipped over the center 27 sts, about 5 ½ in / 14 cm long. Crochet the two sides separately.

7. Work 2 rows of dc on each side as follows: At the beginning of each side (neck edge) work 1 sc and then dc across rest of row. Turn as usual (with ch 2) and omit 1 dc when you crochet back. Turn with ch 1, Work sc on the last row of the sleeve. Cut yarn.

Work the other side the same way. The neckline should be about 6 ¼ in / 16 cm wide.

Front

1. Work as for the back until you reach the point of increasing for the sleeves with chain st.

2. Make the chain sts for the sleeves as for the back, but, on the 1st row with dc, crochet only to the center st = beginning of front neck.

3. Work one sleeve as follows:

Rows 1-5: Work in dc without decreasing the stitch count.

Row 6: Dec 1 dc = skip the 1st dc and insert hook into 2nd dc of previous row.

Row 7: Dec 2 dc at neck edge = skip the last 2 dc of previous row and turn with ch 1 for a slight shift.

Row 8: Work 1 dc in the 2nd dc of previous row = skip the 1st dc. See drawing for front neck shaping.

Repeat rows 7 and 8 until the front is same length as back.

4. I worked in sc across the last row without any shaping. The front neckline now looks like gentling sloping stair steps. If everything has been done correctly, the front and back will meet at the shoulders and the neck widths match. If they don't, you'll need to rip out and readjust the shaping. You might need to decrease more stitches (for example, repeat row 7 several times) or decrease fewer stitches (work row 8 more times).

Finishing

1. Check the yarn ball band for correct iron setting. Steam press the sweater on the wrong side under a damp pressing cloth until garment is nice and smooth.

2. With RS facing RS, sew the front and back together by hand with small stitches. You can use the knitting yarn for seaming but I used a doubled strand of matching sewing thread so that I can make very fine stitches.

Crochet around the Edges

I worked sc rather tightly around the neck and sleeve edges with the same color of yarn as for the sweater and then I worked another round of sc around the sleeve edges with a contrast color. This edging makes a smooth finishing and helps to even out the stair step appearance of the neckline. It is important that the single crochet be worked evenly and that the hook is inserted to the same depth (about ¼ in / .5 cm) into the garment edge so that the stitches will all be the same length. Spray the edging with water and then steam press carefully to make it flat and smooth. It is amazing how smooth crochet work becomes when it is ironed well.

Polka Dots

1. Ch 5 and join into a ring with sl st.

2. Work 2 sc into each chain st around. End rnd with 3 or 4 sl sts for a smooth finishing.

3. Cut yarns and sew on polka dots with matching sewing thread.

   If you want larger circles, work another round with 2 sc into each sc of previous rnd. On rnd 3, you might need to increase only on every other stitch. It depends on how tightly/loosely you crochet. If the circle becomes cornet-shaped, rip it out and work again with more increases. If the circle has wavy edges = rip it out and work again with fewer increases.

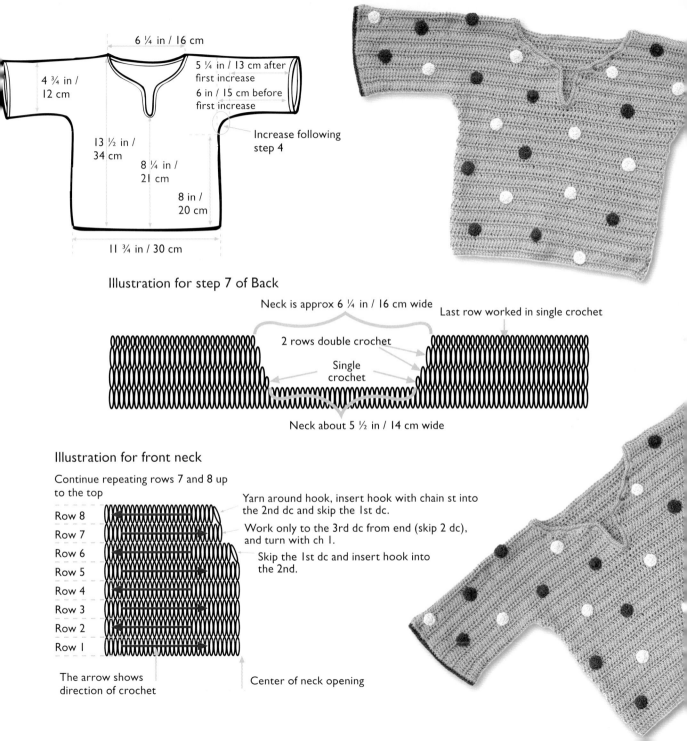

6 ¼ in / 16 cm

4 ¾ in / 12 cm

5 ¼ in / 13 cm after first increase

6 in / 15 cm before first increase

Increase following step 4

13 ½ in / 34 cm

8 ¼ in / 21 cm

8 in / 20 cm

11 ¾ in / 30 cm

Illustration for step 7 of Back

Neck is approx 6 ¼ in / 16 cm wide

Last row worked in single crochet

2 rows double crochet

Single crochet

Neck about 5 ½ in / 14 cm wide

Illustration for front neck

Continue repeating rows 7 and 8 up to the top

Row 8
Row 7
Row 6
Row 5
Row 4
Row 3
Row 2
Row 1

Yarn around hook, insert hook with chain st into the 2nd dc and skip the 1st dc.

Work only to the 3rd dc from end (skip 2 dc), and turn with ch 1.

Skip the 1st dc and insert hook into the 2nd.

The arrow shows direction of crochet

Center of neck opening

Colorful toys are a delight
to make and make wonderful gifts!

Knobbly Ball

Materials:

Several bright colors of cotton yarn (I also used tweeds), crochet hook suitable for yarn (I used US D-3 / 3 mm, sewing needle and matching thread, stuffing (I used old T-shirts to add some weight to the ball—fiber fill is very light and will make it hard for a one-year-old to grip the ball).

Instructions:

1. Ch 2, skip the first ch and work 2 sc into 2nd chain from hook. Turn with ch 1.

2. 2 sc into each st = 4 sts. Turn with ch 1.

3. Work 2 sc into first and last sts and work 1 sc into rem sts = 6 sc.

4. Continue, increasing with 2 sc into first and last sts of row and 1 sc into each of the sts between. Turn each row with ch 1. When there are 18 sts across, work 1 row sc without any increases.

5. Turn with ch 1, skip the first st and sc across to last 2 sts, skip 1 st and then sc into last st = 16 sc.

6. Sc back without any decreases.

7. Rep steps 5 and 6 until 10 sts rem. Work 1 row without decreasing. Cut yarn.

Make a total of 12 pentagon blocks in various colors. Join blocks as shown in drawing but do not sew the two halves together. Sew on the knobs and then finish joining the ball.

Knobs – Crochet the little balls tightly so that the filling won't poke out from any holes.

1. Ch 4 and join into a ring with 1 sl st.

2. Work 6 sc around ring.

3. Work 2 sc into every st around – 12 sc.

4. Rnds 3-4: 1 sc into each st around.

5. End with 1 sl st and cut yarn.

6. Fill the little ball with matching yarn or fiber fill. Tighten circle over filling and sew knobs to ball. **It is very important that the knobs be securely attached to the ball. If your child bites, chews, and puts everything in her/his mouth, you should omit the knobs.**

Joining the blocks

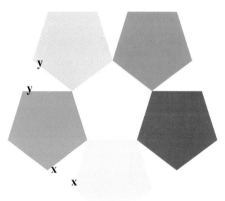

Sew the blocks for the ball together as shown in drawing.

Match x to x and y to y around one half. Join the blocks of the other half of the ball the same way. Now sew the two halves together except for one block. Fill the ball and then join the last block.

Green Striped Dress

Materials:
2 shades of green "Fine Alpaca" (100% alpaca, 182 yds / 167 m per 50 g), and 1 skein pink "Faerytale." (100% alpaca, 191 yds / 175 m per 50 g), A smooth pink mother-of-pearl button, crochet hook US size C / 2.5 mm.

Size:
5-6 years old

Please Read before You Start!
Before crocheting a garment, find a similar one to measure from. If you want to crochet a dress/tunic, get one that fits the child. At every step of the process, check the crochet work against the finished dress. Lay the crochet pieces against the finished garment so that you can verify that the armholes, neck, length, width, etc always match. You can follow my general instructions and increase/decrease as necessary to match the finished garment that fits the intended recipient.

I used a rather fine yarn for this dress and crocheted somewhat loosely so it is difficult to give you precise measurements. If you use a thicker yarn, the stitch count will be totally different.

This dress is 21 in / 53 cm long, 12 ¼ in / 31 cm across body and 17 in / 43 cm at lower edge. **Note:** These measurements are for width, not circumference, and represent only half the total body measurements. See drawing on page 111.

Instructions:
Back and front are worked the same way to neck shaping

1. I began with ch 80 (not counted as row 1); ch 1 to turn. Yarn around hook and insert hook into 3rd ch from hook. Continue in dc across and turn each row with ch 2. Work 4 rows with one color and then change colors.

2. On the 4th row, dec 1 dc = do not work into the last dc of row; turn with ch 2 on second-to-last st.

3. Row 5: change colors, Dec 1 dc at end of row as for step 2. Work a total of 4 rows in same color.

4. Dec 1 st at end of row 8. Change color and dec 1 st at end of row 9.

5. Dec 1 st at end of row 12. Change color on row 13 and dec 1 dc at end of row.

6. Continue, changing colors every 4 rows and dec as before on rows 20 and 21, 24 and 25. Work straight up to row 34 and work across in dc.

7. Row 35: Turn with ch 1, work 3 sc into the first 3 dc of previous row. Ch 1 and then work in dc until 3 sts remain; work 1 sc and turn with ch 1.

8. Row 36: Sc 2 and then work in dc across until 4 sts rem (3 sc + 1 dc of previous row), work 1 sc.

Front
Row 37: From this point, I worked only with light green yarn.

Count the number of sts (excluding underarm sts). I had 42 dc. Begin at armhole with 2 ch (= 1 dc) and then dc across until 2 sts from center front. Into the 2 sts before center, work 1 sc and 1 sl st.

Sweet as candy this little dress makes a nice fall outfit.

Row 38: Turn without a chain st. I sl st into sc (skipping sl st of previous row). Work 3 sc and then 9 dc (= or as many dc as needed to finish row; it is most important that you work as instructed for neck shaping). Ch 2 and turn.

Row 39: Work across dc (for my tunic, it was 9 dc), and then work 2 sc and 1 sl st. Turn without chaining.

Row 40: I sl st into sc (skip sl st of previous row), 3 sc and 9 dc. Ch 2 and turn.

Row 41: I worked back and forth in dc across the remaining 9 dc for shoulder strap (measure child for shoulder strap length). I worked a total of 8 rows.

Work other side of neck the same way, reversing shaping. Cut yarn.

Back
Row 37: From this point, I only used light green yarn.

Work back and forth in dc (I made 42 dc across) up to row 40.

Row 40: 9 dc, 2 sc, 2 sl sts and turn.

Row 41: 2 sl sts into sc and then 9 dc. Cut yarn.

Make the other back shoulder strap the same way.

Finishing
If necessary, steam press the front and back on the wrong side. Check the ball band for recommended heat setting on iron.

With wrong sides facing, seam the pieces with small stitches. I used a doubled strand of matching sewing thread. Turn tunic right side out.

Embellishments
With light green yarn, work 1 row of sc around neck and armholes. With pink, work a row of sc into the green sc row.

Work the pink edging around lower edge as follows:

Work *2 sc, 1 hdc, 2 dc, 1 tr, 2 dc, 1 hdc; rep from * around. Crochet rather loosely so that the semi-circles don't pull together. They should be round and flat.

Corsage Roses
Make a cord of chain sts about 5 ¼ in / 13 cm long and then work 2 rows of sc into cord. Cut yarn. Roll the cord together somewhat loosely and use matching sewing thread to sew the rolled cord so it looks like a rose.

Waist tie
Chain a cord long enough for the waist and then work 1 row sc across chain. Thread cord through double crochet sts at waist.

Sew on the mother-of-pearl button as a decoration.

Shoulder Strap 1 ½ in / 4 cm

12 ¼ in / 31 cm

17 in / 43 cm

Child's Striped Scarf

Materials:
4 colors of mercerized cotton yarn, knitting needles US size 2 or 3 / 3 mm. For the little balls, turquoise lurex yarn and crochet hook US size A / 2 mm.

Instructions:
Scarf
1. With US size 2 / 3 mm ndls, CO 30 sts.

2. *Work back and forth in stockinette for 2 ¾ in / 7 cm and then change colors. Repeat from * until scarf is desired length. The child's scarf I made is 23 ¾ in / 60 cm long.

3. Binding off: K2, *pass the right st over the left one on right needle, k1; rep from * across. Steam press scarf under a damp cotton pressing cloth until scarf is smooth. Check the ball band for recommended heat setting.

4. Fold the scarf with RS facing RS and then seam with very fine stitches in matching doubled sewing thread. My scarf is 2 ½ in / 6 cm wide. Leave an opening in one of the short ends. Turn scarf right side out.

5. Finish seaming along short end.

Balls
Note: The balls must be crocheted very firmly so that the filling won't poke out.

1. With glittery lurex yarn, ch 4 and join into a ring with 1 sl st.

2. Work 6 sc around ring = do not work into the chain sts but around the ring.

3. Work 2 sc into each sc of previous round = 12 sc.

4. Work 3 rnds with 1 sc into each st.

5. Fill the ball (matching color fiber/yarn) or with the same yarn as for crocheting the ball. You can also use fiber fill but it is usually white and that can be seen through the crochet or poke out through the stitches if you didn't crochet tightly enough.

6. Work 1 sc into every other st around until ball is rounded. Crochet tightly so there aren't any holes between the stitches. Crochet the opening closed and cut yarn; weave in tails securely on WS.

7. Attach the balls very securely at each corner so that they won't fall off. Use a doubled strand of sewing thread, make several knots and attach in a number of places. Leave a long tail so it won't pull out when you trim it. If you have a child who puts everything in his/her mouth, don't put the balls on.

Little Boys also enjoy dressing up!

Child's Crocheted Circle Belt

Materials:
Multi-color tweedy cotton yarn and crochet hook suitable for yarn.

Instructions;

1. Ch 5 and join into a ring with 1 sl st.

2. Increase by working 2 sc into each chain around.

3. I worked 2 sc into approx every other sc in previous round (that is, 2 sc into next sc and then 1 sc into following sc) as that worked well with my crochet tension. If that rate of increase doesn't work for you, you can adjust it as follows: if the piece is a "bowl-shaped" circle, you need to increase more often = work 2 sc into more sts around; if the circle is wavy, you need to work fewer increases.

4. When the circle is large enough, end with 4-5 sl sts on the last row for a rounded finish. My circles are 2-2 ½ in / 5-6 cm in diameter. Make as many circles as needed to go around the child's waist

5. Sew the circles to each other and then make 3 cords of varying lengths. Attach the cords to the first and last circles so you can tie the belt. To make the belt smoother, steam press it well.

A decorative belt that's very easy to make.

Scarf with Decorative Flowers & Butterflies

Materials:
"Fine Alpaca" (100% alpaca, 182 yds / 167 m per 50 g), (I used 5 colors), crochet hook US size C / 2.5 mm, sewing needle and matching thread for attaching the hanging objects.

Instructions:
Shell Pattern
1. Ch 38, turn, *1 sc, skip 2 ch, work 5 dc into the next ch, skip 2 ch; rep from * across and end with 1 sc.

2. Change colors (change colors after every row). Turn with ch 3, work 2 dc into sc of previous row, 1 sc into each of next 3 dc, 5 dc into next sc. End row with 3 dc and turn with ch 1. Work 5 dc into the next sc, etc. I worked 24 rows in shell pattern or for about 6 ¼ in / 16 cm.

Single Color section
3. In order to straighten the rows after the shell pattern, work as follows: With the color desired for single color section (in my case, green), Ch 3 + 2 dc. Into the sc of the previous row, work 3 dc (not 5 as before). Work as set across and turn with ch 2 and work in dc. I increased 6 dc evenly spaced across the first row. Make sure that the scarf is straight across. You might need to increase or decrease more stitches than I did.

4. Now continue back and forth with the same color (green, in my case) in dc to the middle of the scarf. I worked 18 ¼ in / 46 cm in double crochet.

5. Make the other side of the scarf as for the first, beginning with shell pattern, changing color when you reach the double crochet section. I used cerise. This side also had 18 ¼ in / 46 cm in single color double crochet. Firmly join the two sections at the middle with single crochet.

6. With a contrast color, work a row of sc all around the scarf. As you work the sc, catch and cover any loose tails so the scarf won't unravel.

Objects
Butterfly body: Ch 10 and work in sc around both sides of the chain cord (see photo) – this book has several illustrations of this. After working around the chain cord, finish with 1 sl st at the top of the "body."

Circles to form the wings: You'll need to make 2 circles for each side of the body. Ch 5 and join into a ring with 1 sl st. Work 2 sc into each chain around. This completes a small circle. With matching sewing thread, sew the parts of the butterfly together with fine stitches. Crochet a little cord for attaching the butterfly to the scarf. Sew cord to scarf edge.

If you want larger circles for the other objects, increase into the previous rounds of sc. The number of stitches you need depends on how loosely/tightly you crochet. Experiment! If you crochet tightly, you'll need to increase more often; increase less if you crochet loosely. Finish each circle with 2-4 sl sts for a smooth edge.

Flower: Crochet a circle following the instructions above until it is desired size. Make the flower petals as follows: Insert hook into a sc in the circle and then ch 5-8 (the number depends on how big you want each flower petal to be), insert the hook into another sc (say, 2 sc over) and make 1 sl st;

A cozy scarf for those cool autumn days.

make a new petal with 5-8 ch. Attach the petals to the circle at even intervals around. Make as many petals as there is room for. Finish with a row of sc around each chain loop and 1 sl st between each petal. Cut yarn and weave in tails on WS. Crochet a little chain cord to hang the flowers on and sew to edge of scarf.

Scarf with Pompoms

Materials:
Yarn for the scarf and crochet hook suitable for yarn, slightly heavier yarn in several colors for the pompoms, cardboard, scissors, sewing needle and matching thread.

Instructions:
1. Ch 25. Turn and, with yarn around hook, insert hook into 3rd ch from hook, make 1 dc. Make 2 more dc in the same chain. Ch 1, *insert hook into the 3rd ch and make 3 dc into that st, ch 1 and rep from * across.

2. Turn with ch 4. Skip the next 3 dc and work 3 dc around the chain loop of previous row. Ch 1 and then work 3 dc into next ch loop. Rep dc groups and ch 1 across, ending with ch 1 and 1 dc into corner of the first dc corner (= at end of row) of previous row. Turn with ch 4 = 1st dc of next row.

3. Continue the same way until scarf is desired length. My child's scarf is 23 ¾ in / 60 cm long.

Pompoms
Draw two circles about 2 in / 5 cm diameter on some thin cardboard or card stock. Cut a hole in the center of each circle about 1 in / 2.5 cm across. Hold the circles together and wind the yarn through the holes. It will go faster if you use doubled or quadrupled strands of yarn. Continue until the hole at the center is completely full. Part the yarn so you can find the cardboard inside. Insert the tips of sharp scissors between the two circles and cut the yarn all around the circles. Wrap some strong thread between the two circles and tie firmly together so that the pompom holds together. Leave a tail so you can tie the pompom to the scarf. Remove the cardboard circles and shape the pompom between your palms (as if rolling round cookies). Trim the yarn evenly all around with sharp scissors.

Tip: Mix the colors of the yarn for the pompom for a tweedy look.

> I enjoy making children's clothes, you can add pompoms for a fun touch and have the children help you make them.

Pin for a Hat

Materials
Half bleached cotton yarn, two kinds of smooth lurex yarn, matching beads, sewing needle and thread.

Instructions
1. Ch 4 and join into a ring with 1 sl st.

2. Increase by working 2 sc into each stitch around on the first 2-3 rounds. Now you'll have to decide how much to increase. Usually 1 extra st into every other st works well. If the circle is big enough, end with 3-4 sl sts for an even finishing of the circle. Cut yarn when you want. I worked 3 rounds with the first yarn and then 1 rnd with the turquoise lurex yarn and 1 rnd with brown lurex yarn.

3. Sew some smooth beads onto the brooch and then sew a safety pin to the back or sew the pin directly onto the hat.

Heart for a Sweater

My children frequently get holes and stains on their clothes…and it's certainly not environmentally friendly to throw the garments into the garbage instead of fixing them. So, here's what I came up with to save the garment.

Materials:
Yarn (my heart is a bit large but that is because I used heavy yarn). If you use thinner yarn, you'll get a smaller heart. Crochet hook suitable for yarn; if desired, mohair yarn for a decorative edge around the heart.
Tip: If you work with wool yarn, the heart will be more even than with a smooth cotton yarn that can leave gaps between the stitches that won't close up if you crochet unevenly.

Instructions:
1. Ch 4 and join into a ring with 1 sl st.

2. Ch 3 (= the first dc), and then work 3 dc around ring = do not work into the chain sts but around them. Ch 1 and turn with ch 1.

3. Work 2 hdc into the first dc, 2 hdc, and then 2 hdc into the last dc = 6 hdc. Ch 1 and turn with ch 1.

4. Work the next 4 rows as for row 3. After completing these rows, there should be 14 hdc across. Turn with ch 1.

5. Work I sc, I hdc, I dc, 3 tr into the next hdc, I dc, I hdc, I sc = center, I sc, I hdc, I dc, 3 tr into next hdc, I dc, I dc, I sc, turn.

6. Work 2 sc, (2 sc into next st) 2 times, 2 sc, 2 sl sts and cut yarn. Turn heart and make the other half the same way.

7. Now use another yarn to crochet around the heart. Begin at the point at the bottom and work in sc up and around. To make a large heart fuller, work 2 sc into each sc of previous row in as many places as necessary so the heart will be rounded at the top (I had to increase 3 sts at the top of each half). At the center (between the two halves of the heart), work I sl st. Make sure that the heart remains flat. Work around the other half of the heart the same way, working in sc down to the point and finish with I sl st. Note: As you are crocheting the edging, catch and cover any loose ends.

Pull the heart into shape with your fingers and steam press on the wrong side so it looks perfect before you sew it onto the garment.

Flowers for a Knit Sweater

Materials:
Assorted colors of leftover yarns matching sweater to be decorated with flowers, crochet hook suitable for yarn, sewing needle and matching thread.

Instructions:

1. Ch 4 and join into a ring with 1 sl st.

2. Ch 6 and work 1 dc around ring. *Ch 3, 1 dc around ring. Rep from * until there are 6 dc around ring. Ch 3 and join to top of first dc (that is, the 4th ch).

3. Work flower petals as follows: into each chain loop around, work 1 sc, 1 hdc, 3 dc, 1 hdc, 1 sc .

4. Sew the flowers randomly onto the sweater.

Make an old sweater look like new with some pretty flowers!

Many warm thanks to Kari Hestnes for the unbelievably beautiful alpaca yarn from "Du Store Alpakka." For more about the yarns, see her webpage: www.dustorealpakka.com. You can also visit the shop in Oslo.

A big thanks also to my beloved family! Alice and Nils – you are the world's best children as well as brilliant and patient models! Thanks also to the two little sisters Astrid and Ebba who were so wonderful in front of the camera. And last but not least thanks to my husband, Casper, who was disappointed because he didn't get a single scarf...

Frida

On the next pages you'll fine Frida's easy crochet and knitting schools. ▷

Chain stitch (ch st)

I. Begin chain st with a slip knot as shown above, tightening it just enough so that it stays on crochet hook.

2. Yarn around hook and pull it through the loop on hook as shown in drawing.

3a. Make a series of chain sts for a chain st cord or beginning chain.

3b. This drawing shows how to bring the yarn through for a new chain st.

Slip stitch (sl st) and Around the Ring

Slip stitch:
Pull yarn through both loops on the hook so only I loop remains.

b. When joining a chain into a ring, work the slip st as follows: yarn around hook and pull through both loops on hook so that only I loop remains on hook.

"Around the Ring"
After you've made a chain st ring, work first round by inserting hook into center of ring, go under sts, yarn around hook, and draw hook back through center to form stitches which will sit over the chain st ring.

Single Crochet (sc)

1.

Make a chain st cord and turn; insert hook into the second ch from hook and catch the yarn as shown in drawing.

2.

Yarn around hook and pull through the chain st – two loops now on hook. Yarn around hook again and bring through both loops on hook.

3.

Now only 1 loop remains on the hook. Insert the hook into the next stitch and repeat steps 1-3.

Double and Triple Crochet

Half Double Crochet (hdc):

Yarn around hook; insert hook down through stitch and catch yarn – see drawing. Bring yarn through

stitch = 3 loops on hook. Yarn around hook and bring through all 3 loops on hook. Now you've completed a half double crochet.

Double Crochet (dc):

Yarn around hook and insert hook through stitch and catch yarn – see drawing. Bring yarn through so that you have 3 loops on

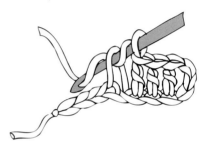

the hook. Yarn around hook and through the first 2 loops; 2 loops remain on hook. Yarn around hook and bring through the remaining 2 loops. Now you've completed a double crochet.

Triple (also called treble) Crochet (tr):

Yarn around hook two times and insert hook through stitch (single crochet or beginning chain); catch yarn – see drawing. Bring yarn through so that you have

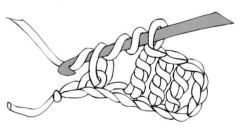

now 4 loops on the hook. Yarn around hook and bring through 2 loops = 3 loops rem. Yarn around and bring through 2 loops = 2 loops rem. Yarn around hook and bring through remaining loops. Now one loop remains and you've completed a triple crochet.

Knitting – Knit and Purl Stitches

Stockinette Stitch / Right Side   **Wrong Side**

Knit Stitch Step 1:
Insert the right needle into the first stitch, bring yarn behind the left needle and bring through to the front.

Knit Stitch Step 2:
Slip the new stitch over to the right needle.

Purl Stitch Step 1:
Pull down the top yarn with the left thumb and pull it through the stitch with the right needle.

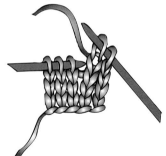

Purl Stitch Step 2:
When you have a new stitch on the right needle, pull the left needle out of the new stitch.

Knitting – Casting On with Long-Tail Cast-On

Casting On Step 1:
Make the first stitch with a slip knot as shown in drawing. Pull on yarn tails so that stitch sits nicely around both needles held together. Make sure that the yarn is long enough for the number of stitches you need to cast on.

Casting On Step 2:
When you've tightened the first stitch, hold the yarn as shown in the drawing.

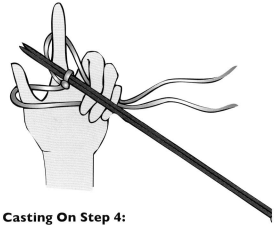

Casting On Step 3:
Catch the "thumb" yarn (nearest you) with the needle. Catch the index finger yarn (furtherest to left) and pull it under the thumb thread. Slip the thumb yarn off and tighten stitch by pulling on both tails slightly. Now you have a new stitch.

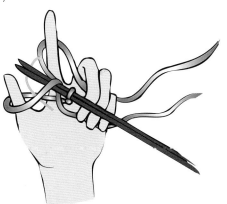

Casting On Step 4:
This is how your stitches should look when you've cast on with long tail cast-on.

Pull out one knitting needle and begin working on the WS with purl stitches for stockinette knitting.

ABBREVIATIONS

beg	begin/beginning
BO	bind off
ch	chain
cm	centimeter(s)
cn	cable needle
CO	cast on
dc	double crochet
dec	decrease
hdc	half double crochet
in	inch(es)
inc	increase
k	knit
k1f&b	knit into front and then back of stitch (= 1 st increased)
mm	millimeter(s)
p	purl
rep	repeat
rnd(s)	round(s)
RS	right side
sc	single crochet
sl	slip
st(s)	stitch(es)
tr	triple or treble crochet
WS	wrong side
yds	yards

YARN SUPPLIERS

For help choosing a suitable yarn contact one of the suppliers below or your local yarn shop for help. The internet is also a great tool for help finding yarn.

USA

Halcyon Yarn
800-341-0282
www.halcyonyarn.com
service@halcyonyarn.com

Webs – America's Yarn Store
800-367-9327
www.yarn.com
customerservice@yarn.com

Norway

Du Store Alpakka
www.dustorealpakka.com

Available from Du Store Alpakka

Babysilk: 80% baby alpaca, 20% silk, 145 yds / 133 m per 50 g

Faerytale: 100% alpaca, 191 yds / 175 m per 50 g

Fine Alpaca: 100% alpaca, 182 yds / 167 m per 50 g

Mirasol: 100% alpaca, 137 yds / 125 m per 50 g

Misti: 100% alpaca, 55 yds / 50 m per 50 g

Nanuk: 100% alpaca, 44 yds / 40 m per 50 g

17.95   3/6/12.